ADVENTUROUS PUB WALKS

IN

NORTHUMBERLAND

Stuart Miller

COUNTRYSIDE BOOKS

NEWBURY BERKSHIRE

COUNTRYSIDE BOOKS
3 Catherine Road
Newbury, Berkshire

To view our complete range of books,
please visit us at
www. countrysidebooks co.uk

ISBN 978 1 84674 183 8

Designed by Peter Davies, Nautilus Design

Produced through MRM Associates Ltd., Reading
Typeset by Jean Cussons Typesetting, Diss, Norfolk
Printed in Thailand

CONTENTS

AREA MAP SHOWING THE LOCATION OF THE WALKS

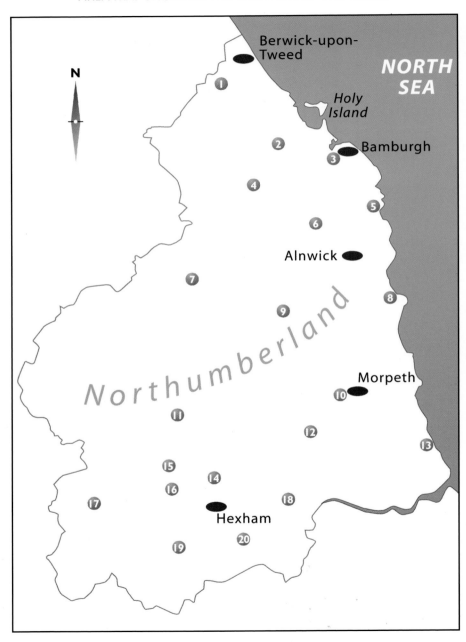

INTRODUCTION

The essence of *Adventurous Pub Walks* is not that you have to gamble on whether the pub is closed when you get there or that the food is cold. No, these are adventurous because they will lift you out of everyday life and let you escape for the day into the depths of one of the largest, most beautiful and least populated counties in England, and also one of the most interesting in historical terms.

The average length is about 11 miles – enough to stretch your legs, build up a good appetite and leave you exhilarated. Many of them, though, do allow you to choose shorter alternative routes if you need to (four of them – Allendale, Embleton, Old Bewick and Norham – are actually near figure-of-eight routes). Several of the walks take you into very remote parts of Northumberland – the vast Kielder Forest is just about the nearest you can get to wilderness in this country. The recommended paths and rights of way are all regularly used and are clearly defined on good maps – although it should be emphasised that the term 'right of way' does not necessarily imply that there is actually an obvious path. In some cases there are stretches of road walking and you should always be traffic-aware but, as far as possible, these routes are along quiet lanes and minor roads. One walk, Shillmoor/Alwinton, does have a short stretch above the Coquet Gorge which is not suitable for people who suffer from vertigo or for small children but the path is clear and regularly used, and there is an alternative road section. The cantankerous, but shallow, Forest Burn which you may encounter on the Simonside/Rothbury walk must be crossed on (supposed) stepping stones repeatedly but it is wet rather than dangerous. Again there is an alternative quiet lane route for the faint-hearted.

Northumberland is a county of superlatives. Next to Yorkshire, which doesn't count really because it is divided administratively, Northumberland is the largest and most northerly county of England. Much of it is further north than parts of south-west and central Scotland because of the oblique nature of the border. The border took centuries to develop. The ancient Saxon kingdom of Northumbria once extended as far north as East Lothian. For a short period Scottish kings ruled as far south as North Tynedale, and sleepy Wark was briefly a settlement of great significance. For 300 years Northumberland was fought over by the English and Scots, officially and unofficially, until in 1603 the uniting of the two crowns ended division and the 'debatable lands' were no longer under debate. As a result of this bloody past the county also has one of the highest densities of castles and fortified houses in the country. On many of these walks you will discover peles, bastles and great castles and the names of some of the great and more lowly families who built them. Indeed, many of the names of the lordly families of Northumberland, such as Waterford and Tankerville, are embodied in the names of inns which appear on these routes.

Northumberland also possesses a lovely coastline with superb beaches. It is well known as Northumberland's 'Lordly Strand'. No decent sandcastle builder worth the name should bypass Embleton, Bamburgh or Alnmouth beaches which all figure as sections of walks in this book. The great artist J.M.W. Turner may not have built many sandcastles. He probably consumed Craster's famous kippers. He certainly became obsessed with the Northumbrian coastline and castles. He painted Dunstanburgh Castle on numerous occasions in varying light using a studio in Embleton.

One of the key attractions of Northumberland is the Roman Wall World Heritage Site which is also a long-distance trail. On two of these walks, Brocolitia and Bardon Mill, you will encounter the wall with its network of fortresses, milecastles and ditches and you will also meet the mysterious dark Cult of Mithras, and another remarkable worldwide organisation.

Northumberland is also a land of paradox. Amidst modern arcadian scenery you will find areas which were once significant industrial landscapes. Comely Allendale was once the lead capital of Britain. The lower Tyne valley of engraver Thomas Bewick was covered in a network of waggon ways carrying coal along its banks to rendezvous with colliers in Newcastle harbour. Seaside Seaton Sluice was the focus of a huge industrial complex of glass and bottle manufacturing. Bardon Mill has its famous pottery, from which one walk starts. Even sleepy Embleton was once a quarrying centre. On many of these walks you will encounter areas which nowadays give little indication of their industrial past. Similarly, you will find that long-since abandoned railways are now attractive trails for walkers and cyclists.

Today, Northumberland is becoming one of the most rapidly developing tourist attractions in England. In recent studies it has been identified as the most tranquil, the least densely-populated, the least spoilt, the least light-polluted county in England. If there was a league table for friendliness, Northumbrians would probably top that as well. Daniel Defoe, that indefatigable 18th-century tourist, government spy and brilliant novelist, once had a guided tour up the Cheviot and claimed that it was possible to see the white sails of the colliers on the Tyne. This is often used as evidence of the air's clarity in 18th-century England – but Defoe was prone to imaginative exaggeration and most of the colliers standing in the Tyne would hardly have their sails set. Nevertheless, Northumberland is a place with clearer air than most. If you do the Wooler and Shillmoor walks you can at least skirt the Cheviots, test the air and enjoy good views across them.

With one exception these walks are designed so that you will encounter an inn or inns on the way round. In each case, an inn has been singled out and recommended but there will be alternatives. Northumberland is rich in characterful inns and public houses. Given the sheer scale of Northumberland, and the significance of routes through the county between England and Scotland, inns have played an important role in the history of the area. Many of them such as the Rose and Thistle in Alwinton and the Twice Brewed near the Roman wall have intriguing stories themselves. There is one exception. The area north of Belsay is short of inns, partly because the Blackett-Trevelyans of Wallington Hall were staunch supporters of temperance. However, there are no fewer than three good coffee shops on the Bolam route, so that walk is a special *Adventurous Coffee Shop Walk*. It is also one of the most historical.

Of course you should go well equipped on walks of this length. Have the appropriate OS maps and a compass with you – and know how to use them. Carry spare warm clothing, and good waterproofs because it rains occasionally in Northumberland! Take plenty of drink and also be prepared to picnic in some sequestered magic dell if you miss opening time at the inn.

Enjoy these walks. Enjoy Northumberland.

Stuart Miller

PUBLISHER'S NOTE

*W*e hope that you obtain considerable enjoyment from this book; great care has been taken in its preparation. Although at the time of publication all routes followed public rights of way or permitted paths, diversion orders can be made and permissions withdrawn.

We cannot, of course, be held responsible for such diversion orders and any inaccuracies in the text which result from these or any other changes to the routes or any damage which might result from walkers trespassing on private property. We are anxious though that all details covering the walks are kept up to date and would therefore welcome information from readers which would be relevant to future editions.

The simple sketch maps that accompany the walks in this book are based on notes made by the author whilst checking out the routes on the ground. However, for the benefit of a proper map, we do recommend that you purchase the relevant Ordnance Survey sheet covering your walk. The Ordnance Survey maps are widely available, especially through booksellers and local newsagents.

TWIZEL BRIDGE, NORHAM AND THE TWEED

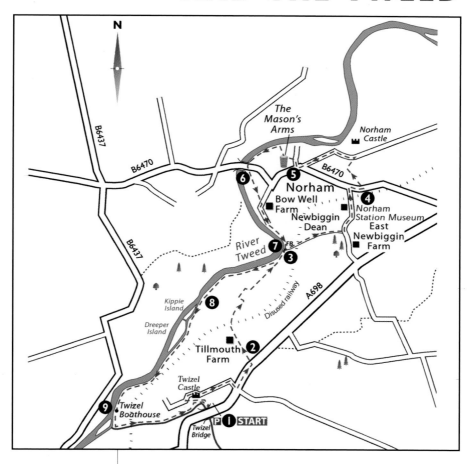

Distance:
11 miles

Map: OS Explorer 339 Kelso, Coldstream & Lower Tweed Valley

Starting Point:
Twizel Bridge.
GR 885433

How to get there: *Twizel Bridge is 5 miles south-west of Norham on the A698 Coldstream–Berwick road. Park in the small area at the east end of Twizel Bridge.*

THE MEDIEVAL TWIZEL BRIDGE

*T*his is a figure-of-eight walk with a great northern castle at one end and the mock-medieval, 18th-century Twizel Castle at the other. Much of it is along the banks of the Tweed, with a long section through thick woods rising high above the river as you approach the junction of the Till and the Tweed and the famous medieval Twizel Bridge, which played a significant role in the events leading up to the momentous Scottish disaster at Flodden Field.

The **Mason's Arms** in Norham is a small local, with genuine character. Dominating the decorations, inevitably, are fishing rods. There is a real fire in the intimate public bar in winter and a small restaurant. The main beers are Belhaven and Deuchars. There is a range of excellent home-made soup (advertised as 'a meal in itself'). Main courses include substantial home-made courses such as Mick's grill, sausage and liver casserole and honey roast pork. There is also a range of sandwiches and a small sweets menu.

The Mason's Arms is open from 11 am to 11 pm. Food is served from 12 noon to 2 pm and from 7 pm to 8.30 pm. No food is served on Sunday evenings. Dogs are allowed in the bar.

Telephone: *01289 382326*

 The Walk

1 From the small parking area go back through a gate and follow a public footpath on the right, signed to **Twizel Castle**. Climb the hill and follow the path as it bears left. Then cross a ladder stile into a field. Turn left and walk on past the ruins of the 18th-century **Twizel Castle**. Beyond the ruins bear right to exit onto a minor road via a stile. Turn right along the road to a junction with a main road with **Twizel Smithy** on the right. Turn left along this fast road for a few hundred yards to the entrance of **Tillmouth Farm** and a fingerpost sign saying 'Tillmouth Farm/River Tweed'.

The impressive pile of Twizel Castle is the ruin of an uncompleted mock-medieval castle. Forty years were spent on it by Sir Francis Blake in the late 18th century. Within it are the remains of an old pele tower.

2 Go up the road, past bungalows, to the farm. Follow waymarkers and stiles by wide gates through the farm area to a waymarked track ahead. Keep on into a field passing the remains of a dismantled railway track. Bear diagonally right over the field (or follow the right edge round if it is planted) to cross a ladder stile. Turn left and, after a few yards, turn right to cross the field with a newly-planted hedge on the left. Ahead of you are the buildings and silo of **West Newbiggin Farm**. Cross a waymarked stile and keep on with the hedge on the right now. At the hedge end keep straight ahead with a fence on the right to cross a stile onto a farm track. Now follow the track to go through a metal gate and walk on a few yards to footpath signs. Take the left path marked as 'Riverside Path' and walk on to a waymarked post. Cross a plank bridge to reach a footbridge which links this figure of eight.

3 Cross the footbridge and now turn right. At the path junction go left through a broken gate. Bear left (waymarked) beyond this and climb up steps to another junction at the top of the wood. Turn right and walk along **Newbiggin Dean**, beneath a railway viaduct. Cross a stile (signed back to West Newbiggin) and at a path fork take the right fork (signed 'East Newbiggin') which leads high above woods to a lane. At the lane turn left and walk on, past the former **Norham Station** (now a private museum with limited opening hours) and between the piers of the old railway bridge until you come to a junction at the end of the lane.

4 At the junction of the lane with the B6470 turn right and then soon turn left through an opening onto a bridleway (signed 'Norham Castle'). Cross a footbridge and go through a wicket gate and then follow the left edge of the field to the left corner with a brook to your left. Go through a wicket gate into a wood. Continue on to cross a bridge to the left into a field. In the field turn right and follow the edge of the field to exit by a field gate (signed back to Morrishall Farm) on a lane. Turn left here and walk past the entrance of **Norham Castle** and then down the bank into **Norham**.

Norham Castle was a favourite subject for the artist Turner. Built in 1158 it guarded a key ford over the Tweed. For many years it and the village were an enclave belonging to the Bishop of Durham and not part of Northumberland. The area was known as Norhamshire. This was where Edward I declared himself

Paramount King of Scotland. The castle was involved in a number of sieges and campaigns and figures in the poem **Marmion** *by Sir Walter Scott. There is a Marmion Gate. The large and very grand St Cuthbert's church is the English church closest to Scotland, and was intended to make a statement. The church and castle were both designed by the same architect for Bishop Puiset, one of the Prince Bishops of Durham. This quiet village has very much the appearance and feeling of being Scottish.*

5 To return to the walk turn left out of the **Mason's Arms** and walk to the village green. Turn left there and walk along **Pedwell Way** past a sign to **Ladykirk Bridge** and **Twizell Bridge** and on to **St Cuthbert's church**. Enter the graveyard by a double gate (signed 'The Tweed'). Walk through the churchyard on a grassy path between gravestones passing behind the north side of the church. To the right of a 'No Public Right of Way' sign enter an enclosed path down to the **Tweed**. Turn left and follow the river upstream to **Ladykirk** and **Norham Bridge**. Continue on the same side of the river through a kissing gate and then beneath the bridge and cross a stile on your left.

6 Turn right over the stile and walk along the field edge. As

THE REMAINS OF THE 12TH-CENTURY NORHAM CASTLE

you approach **Bow Well Farm** cross a stile to the right, then follow the path down a wooded bank and out through a wicket gate onto a lane. Turn right and when the lane ends pass through a wicket gate (signed 'Twizell Bridge') and continue over pasture in front of a cottage (past a couple of thoughtful stone nymphs) and then through a field gate into a wood. The path continues by the river. You reach the end of **Newbiggin Dean** and a multi-way marker post at a junction of paths and a familiar footbridge.

7 Cross the footbridge and then bear right, following the path over a plank bridge. Where the path divides, take the right path down steps and across another plank bridge to a Twizel Bridge sign by a ladder stile. Keep on in the same direction along the riverbank, crossing a couple of ladder stiles and passing a couple of fishermen's huts (pass in front of the second one, don't turn left up a grass track). Stay close to the bank side. After the second hut the path becomes quite narrow and there is a steep bank to the right. Cross a ladder stile into woods.

8 Follow the widening path through the woodland. Keep an eye out for giant hogweed. The waymarked path climbs then descends to the riverbank, and then goes through a new plantation. Cross a plank bridge and stay with the undulating path between trees, helped by occasional sections of steps and footbridges. The islands you can see are **Kippie** and **Dreeper**. Following a substantial footbridge the path climbs high above the river. Note the grand house across the river. Keep right at a waymarked post to pass a brick house on the left and reach a public footpath sign to **Twizel Bridge**. Follow the broad path which swings right, back to the river. Keep on to **Twizel Boathouse** along this very pleasant open stretch passing another fishing shiel.

9 Go through a stile to the right of **Twizel Boathouse** and follow the path until you reach the meeting of the waters of the **Till** and the **Tweed**. The ruins opposite are of **St Cuthbert's chapel** built in the 18th century on the site of a much older one. Now the path is a wide grassy one running beside the **Till**. It passes beneath the arches of a bridge which carries the dismantled railway over the river. Keep on to a metal gate. Go through this to reach the old medieval **Twizel Bridge**, with the modern road bridge visible through its arch.

The famous medieval Twizel Bridge across the 'sullen Till' was crossed by the apprehensive 'second eleven' English vanguard on its way to an astonishing victory at Flodden in 1513. Built by the local Selby family, it is a lofty semi-circular, five-ribbed arch with a 90 ft span and a height of 46 ft. The name Twizel *is derived from an Old English word* twisla *which means a place where waters meet, or the addition of a tributary to a main stream. St Cuthbert's chapel at Ladykirk was built by James IV to fulfil a vow made when he nearly drowned in the Tweed. It was the scene of a miracle when the keys were lost in the river and St Cuthbert appeared in a vision to tell the priest to feel inside the mouth of the next salmon caught from the river.*

 Date walk completed:

HOLBURN, ST CUTHBERT'S CAVE, BELFORD AND KYLOE WOOD

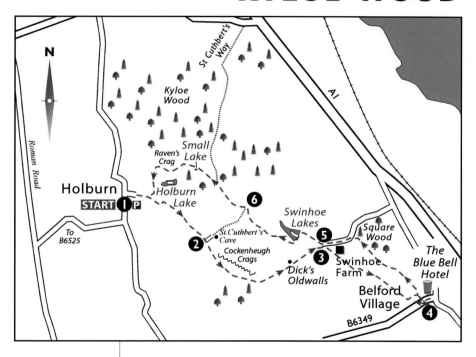

Distance:
11 miles

Starting Point:
Holburn.
GR 042362

Map: OS Explorer 340 Holy Island & Bamburgh

How to get there: *Holburn is north-west of Belford between the B6525 and the B6349. You can park on the side of the lane at East Holburn where there is a small grassy parking area just beyond the cottages and farm buildings.*

ST CUTHBERT'S CAVE, NEAR THE START OF THE ROUTE

*S*erenity is the word for this walk. It's an easy wander through pleasant woodland and across open grassy moors, with excellent views across Northumberland's 'Lordly Strand' and towards the rolling Cheviots. If you start at the quiet little hamlet of Holburn, you will be able to visit the Blue Bell Hotel at the halfway point. This old coaching inn figured in an intriguing story about a 17th-century highwaywoman. However, the main feature of this walk is the famous St Cuthbert's Cave where the remains of the great Northumbrian were rested at the start of a journey of nearly 100 years, following a Viking attack on Lindisfarne.

The family-run **Blue Bell Hotel** is an ivy-covered, former coaching inn standing on what used to be the Great North Road or A1 in Belford. It has a public bar (with a wood fire), restaurant and buttery. One of the inn's great features is the landscaped beer garden with children's play area and views over the countryside. Main beers are Black Sheep, Timothy Taylor's, Tetley's and Calder's. A good range of food is available – Whitby whole-tail scampi, steak and ale pie, steamed mussels in Lindisfarne mead, Northumberland lamb shank, Eyemouth cod and haddock, fish pie and so on. Food is locally sourced.

The Blue Bell is open from 11 am to 12 midnight all week. Food is available from 12 noon to 3 pm and 6 pm to 9 pm.

Telephone: *01668 213543*; www.bluebellhotel.com

 The Walk

❶ Walk through **Holburn** past **East Holburn** and turn right through a wide gate onto moorland. From here just follow the pleasant green track alongside a fence with excellent views over the **Cheviots** to the right. The track bends to the left following the fence then bends right again. It goes through gorse and for a while there is another fence on the left. You pass a stile and gate on the right but keep on. Where the path forks, keep right. Now you reach the woods of **St Cuthbert's Cave**. Go through a wide gate with a stile and walk ahead a few yards then left up the avenue to the famous cave.

It is believed that St Cuthbert's remains rested here for a short while at the start of a long journey which eventually ended at Durham. The great overhanging rock at the front is supported by a natural pillar.

The entrance was once closed by a stone wall. In front of the cave is a huge split boulder with a natural cross formed by weathering. Near this is a man-made niche which might have held a lamp. There is an alternative story that Cuthbert retired here for a time from Lindisfarne in AD 676, rather than to the rocky islet of St Cuthbert's Island.

❷ From the cave, return down the avenue to the track, then turn left to exit from the wood via a stile to the left of a gate. The path continues around the edge of the trees, passing the extravagantly eroded **Cockenheugh Crags** on the left, before coming to a gate that allows you to leave the plantation. Follow a broad track with a stone wall to your right. The wall is later replaced by a wire fence. You go over another ladder stile and keep on. You pass to the left of a small plantation and to the right of the next one. The track takes you past some stone buildings,

17

which are known as **Dick's Oldwalls**. Ahead of you are the buildings of **Swinhoe Farm**.

3 At **Swinhoe Farm**, turn right at a public footpath sign to **Belford**. Pass barns on the right and cottages on the left. Keep on along the drive to the car park of the riding school. Cross this to go through a kissing gate. Stay with the right field edge to cross a stile. Then follow the left field edge to cross another stile and go through a plantation via a gap in a wall. Exit from the plantation into a field across a stile. Keep along the left edge to cross a stile in the corner hidden by gorse. Now turn left and follow the left edge of the next field to cross a stile, then follow a path off to the right. It rises over a bank. Now you can see **Belford** ahead. Keep on as the path passes a marker post and bends right to reach the far left corner of a field. Cross a stone step stile here and follow the left field edge on through a kissing gate, across a little stream and then through another wicket gate. Keep on along the left edge until you come to a kissing gate in the corner. Turn left and then follow a right field edge. You arrive at a stretch of raised stone 'causeway'. Go through a kissing gate and walk on with a little stream below you on the left. Finally, exit through a kissing gate and turn right onto a lane. Follow this down to the main road or **West Street** and turn left past the

Belford Community Club to walk into **Belford** and visit the **Blue Bell Hotel**.

Belford stands on the line of the Great North Road but has now been bypassed. In former times it was very vulnerable to Scottish raids and was described in the early 17th century as 'Belford, nothing like the name either in strength or beauty, is the most miserable, beggarly town, or town of sods, that ever was made in an afternoon of loam and sticks'. However, Belford had a weekly market in the 18th century and two busy annual fairs. The market cross still stands in the old market place. As early as 1416 the 'Castrum de Beleford' stood where West Hall Farm is today. The church of St Mary was rebuilt in 1827 on the site of an ancient chapel. It was just north of Belford where 'Bonny Grizzy' Hume, in male disguise, robbed the carrier of the London mail of the warrant for the execution of her father who was in prison in Edinburgh for his part in a rebellion in 1685. She had tried initially to steal it while he rested at the Blue Bell which was a major coaching inn from 1786 to 1847. Belford was also a famous foxhunting centre. The great sporting journalist Robert Surtees (1805–1864) modelled many of his characters on residents in the area.

4 From the **Blue Bell Hotel** retrace your steps along **West Street** (the B6349 Wooler road) and back up the footpath-signed lane. Pass the familiar kissing gate on the left and keep on, past the castellated building in the field on the left, once the site of the moated Belford Castle but now **Westhall Farm**. To the right are inland-facing cliffs which are typical of this area. At the barns turn left, then right and walk on passing a wartime pillbox on the left. Keep on to **Craggyhall Farm** passing caravans and a brick bungalow. Go through a wide gate and past a limekiln. Keep on beside a dry stone wall on the left and with banks of gorse and broom on the right. At another wide gate ignore the ladder stile on the right and go through into pasture. Now keep to the right field edge until you go through a wicket gate into mixed woodland. At the junction with a forest ride, turn left and follow it out onto a road. Turn left and walk past **Swinhoe Farm** to arrive at a signpost to 'Fenwick and Holburn'.

THE POPULAR BLUE BELL HOTEL

5 At the signpost turn right off the road through a wide gate onto a stony track hedged on the left. It follows the edge of the wood at first. You pass **Swinhoe Lakes** on the right (private). The broad track rises and bends and enters the wood. Keep following the track. Exit the woods via a wide gate. The track now skirts a high gorse-covered basalt heugh or crag with a wire fence at the base. At a gate in a wire fence with a signpost pointing back to **Swinhoe Farm** and to **St Cuthbert's Cave**, cross a stile and walk on a few paces to meet a broad farm track. There is an excellent view over the coast and Holy Island from here.

6 Turn left and follow the clear track ahead which is signed to **Holburn**. The gated track bends round to the right and passes the remains of old coal workings. At a fork keep right (ahead). You enter pleasant **Kyloe Wood** via a wide gate. At a three-way signpost, keep ahead for **Holburn**. You pass a silted-up lake on the left. Soon after this pass a wide gate by the side of it and keep on. The scene starts to open out and you are walking along the edge of the woodland. **Holburn Moss** can be seen over to the left. Ahead is **Rabbit Hill**. Keep with the track as it descends slightly and bends to the right taking you past **Raven's Crag**. The track then swings south and through a gate onto a lovely green track with thick bracken and gorse on the left and a stone wall on the right. Holburn begins to come into sight over on the right ahead. The track winds round to the right, skirting a small wood. Go through a wide gate and past **East Holburn** and back into **Holburn**.

The great outcrops of fell sandstone which are so prominent in this area were laid down as sediment at a time when there was a shallow estuary surrounding the Cheviot dome. However, most of the Kyloe Hills are dolerite and were intruded up into the sedimentary layer at a later date.

Date walk completed:

WAREN MILL, SPINDLESTONE HEUGHS, BAMBURGH AND BUDLE BAY

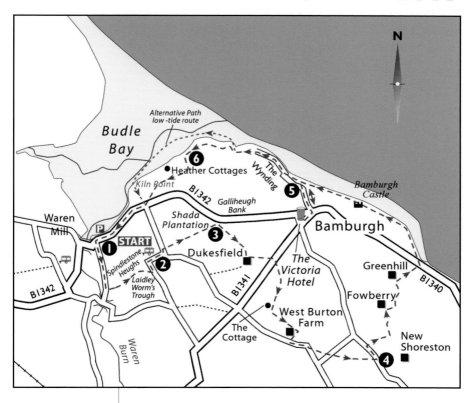

Distance:	Map: OS Explorer 340 Holy Island & Bamburgh
10 miles	

Starting Point:
Waren Mill.
GR 147343

How to get there: *Waren Mill stands 3 miles west of Bamburgh on the B1342 and 3 miles east of the A1. There is roadside parking overlooking Budle Bay.*

21

BAMBURGH CASTLE IN ITS CLASSIC SETTING

A great and ancient castle in a stupendous setting, the famous story of Victorian heroine Grace Darling, the extensive yellow sands of Budle Bay and the strange legend of the Laidley Worm – a dragon with a difference – are just a few features of this walk. For most of it, the horizon is dominated by Bamburgh Castle on its massive basalt rock. The return section of the route is along lovely beaches. There is some road walking along quiet lanes but most of it is over fields.

The ornate and imposing **Victoria Hotel** in Bamburgh was once two private houses built in 1876. It is independently owned and has a very modern Scandinavian wood-panelled interior. There is a spacious lounge decorated with chandeliers and wall mirrors, and a bar and a brasserie. Popular main courses include lamb shank, Bamburgh bangers, and haddock in beer batter. There is also a good range of sandwiches. Beers include Black Sheep and John Smith's.

The Victoria Hotel is open from 10 am to 10 pm on Sunday and until 11 pm on weekdays. Bar meals are available from 12 noon to 8.30 pm and Sunday lunch from 12 noon to 2 pm. The Brasserie restaurant is open daily from 7 pm.

Telephone: *01668 214431*; www.thevictoriahotel.net

 *The Walk*

1 At **Waren Mill** turn down a lane leading south opposite **Waren Lea** and along beside the grounds of the **Waren House Hotel**. Keep on along the wooded lane until you reach a sign for **Drawkiln Hill** on the left. Turn left through a wicket gate. Follow the path up the bank, then along the woodland edge as it curves to the left. Keep on through a wicket gate into pasture. Keep on alongside the main woodland, with a limekiln on the right, to cross a stile hidden at the left end of the facing fence. Keep on through a waymarked gate and along the pasture's left edge to go through another gate. **Spindlestone Heughs** are now on the left above the trees. Keep on through the wood alongside an old wall to another wide gate and go through. You can see a caravan site ahead. The right of way is through a wicket gate on the left and along the edge of the site to exit via another gate to a minor road, but a stile in the far corner of the field enables you to avoid going into the caravan site if you wish and to pass the famous **Laidley Worm's Trough** which is a small depression supposed to be a haunt of the dragon in the story of the Laidley Worm.

The Laidley Worm, an everyday story of evil, jealousy, bloodshed and incest, is linked to the semi-mythical King Ida who was the founder of the Northumbrian royal line and began his reign in AD 547. Following the death of his wife he married a woman who turned out to be a witch. She was jealous of the beauty of her step-daughter and turned her into a dragon which lived at Spindlestone Heughs and devastated the area. However, her brother, the Childe Wynd, fighting abroad, returned via Warenford and rode inland to confront the creature. On meeting the dragon it asked him to kiss it three times to undo the curse. He did so and the beast turned back into his beautiful sister. Together they rode to Bamburgh Castle. In a trial of magical power the wicked queen was turned into a loathsome toad, and cast down the great well in the castle.

2 At the minor road turn left and walk to a junction by the entrance to the caravan site, then walk right. The hill on the right is **Drawkiln Hill**. At a junction with another road turn left for about 20 yards and climb a stone stile on the right marked **Galliheugh Bank**. Follow the path along a right field edge, enjoying excellent views to the north and south. At the end of the field keep on across a stile towards Bamburgh along the left side of a hawthorn hedge, then across a stile to the right of the **Shada Plantation**. Cross a small bank (the end of **Galliheugh Bank**) and descend along the line of spaced Scots pine and gorse. At the field's end cross a stile onto a minor lane leading onto the B1342 up on the left.

The area is dominated by the towering Bamburgh Castle. It was supposedly the Joyous Gard of Sir Lancelot in Malory's Le Morte d'Arthur. Standing on a dramatic basalt outcrop it was the royal seat of the first kings of Bernicia who created the great kingdom of Northumbria which was ruled from here. It would have been made of

timber; the Normans rebuilt it in stone. The well is 150 ft deep and is cut through solid rock. In the 18th century the castle was bought by Nathaniel, Lord Crewe, Bishop of Durham who married Dorothy Forster, daughter of a leading local squire. He founded a charitable trust which did much for the well-being of local people and which still survives. In the late 19th century it was bought as a second home by Lord Armstrong, the 'Great Gunmaker' of Cragside Hall. Recently it was partly converted into residential accommodation.

3 Turn right to **Dukesfield**. Approaching the end of the lane and near the houses go left across a stile. Walk on to the far right corner of the field to cross one stile then another yards beyond. Continue alongside a hedge to a road. Cross this and continue along a green lane opposite. This may be densely overgrown. Eventually reach a cottage and cross a stile beyond on the left. Keep on down a left field edge to exit via a field gate into **West Burton Farm** and turn right through the farmyard to a lane. Turn left along this. After a right bend cross a stile on the left signed to **New Shoreston**. Bear half right across the field to exit across a stile into a lane. Just opposite is another stile signed to **Ingram Lane**. Cross this, then bear half right across one

GRACE DARLING'S MEMORIAL IN ST AIDAN'S CHURCHYARD

field to cross another stile in the far right corner into another field. Keep along the same half-right line to exit across a complex double stile.

4 Turn left along **Ingram Lane**. After a couple of hundred yards reach a gated bridleway signed to **Fowberry** on the right. Follow this round, past a pillbox, to **Fowberry**. At a meeting with a narrow lane, go left to the farm, then turn right before the entrance onto a green track. In the next field through a wide gate follow the left edge round to a gate. Go through the gate, then follow a right-hand wall to a wide double gate which you go through (ignoring the waymarked right of way ahead) then on across the last field to **Greenhill** and on down a lane to the main road. Cross the road and go down a sandy path to the beach. Turn left and follow the sands to **Bamburgh**. Just beyond **Bamburgh Castle**, turn left and follow a path through the dunes up to a lane called **The Wynding**. Turn left along this into the village and then turn right. The **Victoria Hotel** is just past the village green on the south side.

Bamburgh is also noteworthy for its church and for the story of Grace Darling. St Aidan's church is on the site of the Saxon church where St Aidan died in AD 651. Among the many features is a vaulted crypt where relics of St Aidan would have been kept. There is a marble memorial to the Forster brothers erected by their sister Dorothy, who is claimed to have rescued her brother Thomas from Newgate Prison after the abortive Jacobite rising of 1715. In the churchyard is the monument to Grace Darling who, with her father, rowed from the Longstone Lighthouse and rescued the survivors of the SS Forfarshire which was wrecked on the Farne Islands in 1838. The family plot where she is buried is close by. Also to be seen in Bamburgh is the little house where she was born, the house where she died in 1842, and the recently refurbished and extended Grace Darling Museum.

5 To continue the walk, return to **The Wynding** and walk along it to the end near the golf course house and the coastguard station. Look out for the painted **Stag Rock** near the latter. At the golf course gates you have a choice. If the tide is out and conditions are safe, you can descend to the right of the gate on a path to the foot of the grassy slope and walk round on the sands of **Budle Bay** past the little sheltered coves. (If you

do this, at a Lindisfarne National Nature Reserve sign, turn off left up a bridleway past **Kiln Point cottages** and thence via a wicket gate up to the road where you turn right and walk down into **Waren Mill**.) If the tidal conditions are not suitable, go through the wicket gate then follow a line of blue posts on a variously grassy, gravel and sandy track along the edge of the golf course and past **Budle Point**. The path then descends to pass a gun emplacement.

6 At the marker post near the emplacement, turn left to follow the blue posts on up to the 5th tee and leave the golf course via a kissing gate. Keep on ahead past the caravan site on the right then onto a metalled lane with a sign saying 'The Beach'. Keep on to go through **Budle Newtown Caravan Site** and **Heather Cottages**, passing through a wide gate. At a junction turn left then right and through a waymarked wicket gate. Follow the left edge of the field then cross a ladder stile by a gate. Bear right over the field to exit onto the B1342 at **Budle**. Turn right and walk down to **Waren Mill**.

Date walk completed:

CAREY BURN, WOOLER COMMON, WOOLER AND WEETWOOD MOOR

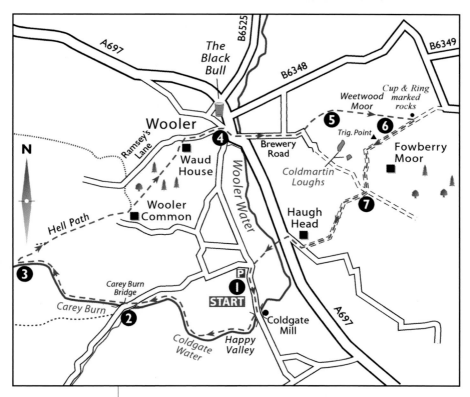

Distance:
12 miles

Starting Point:
North Middleton National Park car park near Wooler. GR 995257

Maps: OS Explorer OL 16 The Cheviot Hills, and OS Explorer 340 Holy Island & Bamburgh

How to get there: *For the North Middleton National Park car park, turn into Wooler off the A697 up Church Street then keep on past the Wheatsheaf towards North Middleton.*

CAREYBURN LINN, SEEN AT POINT 2 OF THE WALK

*T*he outward journey takes you through the well-named Happy Valley and along the banks of the Coldgate Water and the Carey Burn. A brief encounter with Hell Path passes quickly and you return safely over Wooler Common to sample the delights of one of the inns of 'Windy' Wooler. Rested and refreshed you now turn to Weetwood Moor with its strange cup and ring markings and views over the Cheviots and the area through which you walked earlier. A combination of meadows, moors and field edges is involved, with some walking along quiet lanes.

The **Black Bull** in Wooler is a friendly and unpretentious local. Real ales are Young's Waggledance (honey-based) and Secret Kingdom (Hadrian & Border Brewery). There is a good bar meal menu, with a wide range of fish dishes and grills – including the challenging Bull Mixed Grill – as well as a vegetarian selection and a children's menu. The lunch menu also includes breakfasts, jacket potatoes, hot rolls, toasties and sandwiches. There is also the Milan restaurant through the arch (5 pm to 10 pm) serving pastas, pizzas, lasagne and cannelloni. All food is cooked fresh. For the Milan you may need to reserve a table.

The Black Bull is open from 11 am to 11 pm. Food is served from 12 noon to 2.30 pm and 7 pm to 8.30 pm.

Telephone: *01668 283692*

 The Walk

1 From the National Park car park turn right and walk down to a lane. Turn right along this then, at a wood on the right just past **Coldgate Mill**, turn right at a sign to **Harthope Valley** and go through a kissing gate. Stay on this track through the delightful **Happy Valley** to **Carey Burn Bridge** with bubbling **Coldgate Water** on the left. It rises and descends to exit over a step stile into a meadow. Keep on, slightly to the right, then cross another step stile at more woods. Keep along the wood edge with the burn on your left. Cross another meadow keeping on past a marker post at a cross paths. The path rises uphill through bracken and gorse but is obvious enough. It descends into another open area. Follow the grassy path, then cross a stile and keep on into the last meadow area and to a step stile signed back to **Coldgate Mill**. Cross this and turn left along a road to **Carey Burn Bridge**, rebuilt in 1956 to replace one swept away by flooding.

Sir Walter Scott stayed briefly at Langleeford in the Harthope Valley at the foot of the Cheviots where he took the famous 'goat's whey cure' and described an Elysian existence: '[All] the day we shoot, fish, walk and ride; dine and sup upon fish struggling from the stream, and the most delicious heath-fed mutton, barn-door fowls, pies, milk-cheese etc. all in perfection; and so much simplicity resides among these hills, that a pen, which could write at least, was not to be found about the house ... till I shot the crow with whose quill I write this letter.'

William Weaver Tomlinson describes the Coldgate Water (or Wooler Water) as a 'splashing streamlet, fringed with patches of gorse and belts of natural wood – birch, oak, alder, thorn, and mountain ash...' and so it is today.

2 Don't cross the bridge. Cross a step stile at its east end. Follow the **Carey Burn** path up a rocky bank and keep left where a path is met from the right. Ignore side paths as you go into the narrowing valley. The path rises into a scree area, narrows and becomes rocky. Pass the **Careyburn Linn**. Keep on the path across awkward rocky outcrops, past a timber shelter then on towards woodland. Follow the edge of the plantation then enter it via a step stile. The path crosses timber bridges in places then winds round to meet a bridleway (the ominously-named **Hell Path** – probably a corruption of Hill Path) at a T-junction.

3 Turn right and follow the path on through a wicket gate and ahead to a T-junction with a very wide track. Turn right then follow it, crossing three step stiles. Approaching **Wooler Common Farm** turn left over a stile signed 'Brown's Law/Wooler' and follow the wall on the right to cross another stile signed to **Wooler/Waud House**. Turn right and follow a bridleway parallel to the wall through a wide gap in the field corner near a sign to **Waud**

House/Wooler. Aim for the right side of a large plantation to enter it through a wicket gate. Follow the clear woodland path to exit via a gate. Continue on a grassy path passing marker posts. At a fork, turn right on the narrow path and follow it down into the little valley, then through a couple of gates to **Waud House** and a path. Follow the path to exit onto **Ramsey's Lane**. Turn right for **Wooler** centre and the **Black Bull**.

'Windy' Wooler was originally an agricultural market town but developed in the 19th century as the tourist gateway to the Cheviots with their invigorating air. A local doctor wrote a book of walks in 1926 arguing that a holiday at Wooler was a health cure '... capable of being at once a haven of rest and a cornucopia of fresh vigour ...' William Weaver Tomlinson also commented on 'the pure air and water from the Cheviots, and the many attractions of the neighbourhood [which] render the town a favourite resort of persons in delicate health.' But then he spoils it by referring to the 'monotony of life' broken only by markets and fairs!

4 From the **Black Bull** turn left past the bus station then turn left down **The Peth** to the A697, where you turn right and walk alongside the river to the stone road bridge.

Cross this and walk ahead past the **Riverside Bar** on the left and Bridgend chalet and caravan site on the right then along **Brewery Road** past a school on the left. Walk up a bank to a signpost on the left to **Weetwood Moor**. This is also on the route of **St Cuthbert's Way**. From the signpost follow a clear path which winds up easily through bracken, through a wicket gate and into a wildlife conservation area. There are excellent views over Wooler and the Cheviots. All this with little effort! Keep on along the path until you arrive at the top and a waymarked post.

THE WELCOMING BLACK BULL PUB IN WOOLER

5 At the marker post there is a very obvious grassy path ahead and another lesser one bearing to the right. Follow the lesser one. The OS map and the waymarkers tell slightly different stories. Ahead of you over the moor you will see three plantations. Aim for the right-hand end of the middle one. This path will take you there although it gradually diminishes into a much narrower one in thick heather. Keep left at a fork and straight over at a cross paths. Pass small cairns and an isolated waymark post on the right. At the right end of the middle plantation is a gate.

6 Go through the gate and turn right through another gate. Follow a vague path alongside a low ridge

with rock outcrops on your left. On some of those you will find good examples of cup and ring markings. Ahead of you is a patch of gorse and a few trees hiding a signpost and a kissing gate which takes you onto a road. Turn right and walk along the road passing the entrance to **Fowberry Moor Farm** on the left. The road turns in there but keep on along a track. On the right is a trig point and also the Repeater Relay Station. Keep on along the lane/track. You can see **Coldmartin Loughs** in the midst of trees downhill. Go through the left of two gates to stay with your track which turns left here and hugs a plantation on the right until you reach a track junction with excellent views over the Cheviots.

Weetwood Moor is notable for the many cup and ring markings which are particularly associated with Northumberland and the northern area. This 'rock art' takes different forms but the most common design consists of a small hollow surrounded by a number of concentric rings. They date from about 1,600 BC, the period of the early Bronze Age. The meaning of these is obscure. They may have had some religious significance or fertility meaning. Coldmartin Loughs are gradually silting up. A party of foreign mercenaries from Jedburgh raiding the area in the winter of 1548–49 commented upon the phenomenon that the lake never freezes properly even in the coldest weather, 'as several historians have noted'.

7 At this point go through a gate opposite and follow a clearly-defined track down the right field edge. At another track junction don't go ahead but turn left to wind down the track which becomes enclosed on both sides and concrete underfoot. Arriving at a pleasant minor road between high hedges turn right down to **Haugh Head**. At the end of the hedges and approaching barns and cottages turn left down between them to a wicket gate which gives access to the A697. Cross over and follow a lane down, past the old signal box and over **Wooler Water** via an impressive footbridge next to a ford then up to a crossroads. Cross over and return to the car park.

Haugh is common in Northumberland place-names. It means a piece of flat, alluvial land by the side of a river or a meadow. On the other hand a heugh, pronounced in almost the same way, is a ridge or crag.

Date walk completed:

EMBLETON, DUNSTANBURGH CASTLE, CRASTER AND LONGHOUGHTON

CRASTER HARBOUR

Distance:
13½ miles

Map: OS Explorer 332 Alnwick & Amble

Starting Point:
The Dunstanburgh
Castle Hotel in
Embleton.
GR 232225

How to get there: *Embleton is about 7 miles north-east of Alnwick. Turn off on the B6347 from the A1, then follow the B1339 south. You can park in the village centre.*

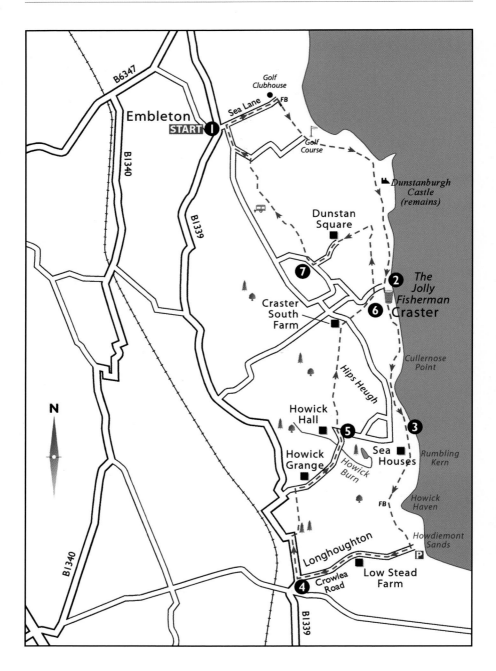

*A*n horizon-dominating, medieval castle is central to this view-ridden coastal walk. The outward section is along beach-edge and cliff-top paths and the return is across pleasant fields. You encounter a family who helped to found modern British democracy, a very practical monument to a casualty in an imperial 'small war', the first 'dunce', and the journalist who established the key principles of modern journalism. Allow enough time to have a crab sandwich and buy smoked kippers in Craster, or to pay a visit to the NAAFI!

The **Jolly Fisherman** in Craster was originally a cottage but became an inn in 1847 when it was opened by a local fisherman. Since then it has been extended. It is dark-panelled and beamed, stone-built and whitewashed – and very authentic. It is split level with a small dining area overlooking the North Sea. There is a small beer garden (through which the route conveniently takes you). Well-known specialities are crab-meat soup, Craster kipper pâté and crab sandwiches. There are also lite bites such as beefburgers and pizzas. A range of desserts is available every day. Black Sheep, John Smith's and Old Speckled Hen are the main beers.

The Jolly Fisherman is open from 11 am to 11 pm. On Sunday it is open from 12 noon to 11 pm. Food is available from 11 am to 2.30 pm, with sandwiches and chips available from 3 pm to 4 pm.

Telephone: *01665 576461*

Note also the Burnside in Longhoughton which is open all day.

 *The Walk*

1 From the **Dunstanburgh Castle Hotel** go up **Front Street** and **Dunstanburgh Terrace** and down **Sea Lane** to the golf course. Pass the clubhouse and go through a wicket gate. Turn right onto the course, skirting round rushes to cross a footbridge on the golf course. Turn right, then follow the waymarked Coast Path along the edge of the course with a hedge to the right. Pass a small copse on the left and the end of a lane. Continue on alongside fenced fields, ignoring a path joining from the left. Follow a waymarked post over the golf course. Go through a kissing gate with a National Trust marker. Continue on towards

Dunstanburgh Castle. Stay on the lower path round the base of basalt crags, past a blockhouse and across a short causeway towards a kissing gate by a wide gate. Go through and continue on to the next fence. Go through another wicket gate next to a wide gate. After the second wicket gate keep on to **Craster**.

Dunstanburgh Castle was built in 1313–1319 by Thomas, Earl of Lancaster as a symbol of his wealth and power, and to match the royal stronghold of Bamburgh at a time when Thomas was a leading opponent of Edward II. There is no keep because the fashion of the day was to put the real strength of a castle into the gatehouse, hence the remains of the great towers. The castle covers an area of 11 acres. Natural features make it a very defendable position. It is particularly photogenic since it changes colour in different lights. J.M.W. Turner returned here frequently to paint it, using a studio at the Sportsman Inn in Embleton.

2 Beyond the harbour at the **Jolly Fisherman** go down the lane on its left, signed Cullernose Point/Coast Path, but then turn right through a wicket gate and through the beer garden to exit via another wicket gate and on along the path which passes the ends of gardens and a children's play area to leave Craster.

Now follow the well-defined gated coastal path round a basalt inlet, then precipitous **Cullernose Point** with its noisy kittiwakes and on, through a wooded patch, to the prominent **Seaview House**.

Craster is a fishing village which developed around a small natural harbour between the rocks of the Little Carr and Muckle Carr. Herring was the basis of its growth. Craster is renowned still for its smoked kippers. The present harbour was created in 1906 in memory of Captain Craster who died in the Younghusband expedition to Tibet in 1904. The large concrete foundation at the end of the south pier formed the bases of two silos used to store whinstone chippings for road building.

3 Keep on past **Seaview House**. At a junction and marker post keep left past the **Rumbling Kern** down the grassy track to cross a stile and keep on. Cross another stile and follow the sandy path. Through a wicket gate carry on along the winding and undulating path. Through a patch of dense gorse and bushes another wicket gate admits you to the little cove of **Howick Haven**. Cross a substantial footbridge and stay with the track past **Sugar Sands** and on to **Howdiemont Sands**. At a beachside car park turn right up a pleasant hedged lane past **Low Stead Farm**. Keep on into **Longhoughton** along **Crowlea Road**.

Just before Howick Haven, up on the right you will see a reconstructed Iron Age hut which can be approached up a path to the right. There was a small settlement here when the sea was further back. It has been excavated by archaeologists. Information boards give a good idea about the lifestyle of the inhabitants.

THE RUINED GATEHOUSE TO
DUNSTANBURGH CASTLE

❹ At a T-junction turn right past the Spar/NAAFI shop then, on the left, the **Burnside**. Just past the last house where the road bends left, follow a footpath sign to the right through a fringe of trees. Turn left at an unsigned path and enter a field. Keep straight over past an old kissing gate into another field. Follow the left edge and pass an old kissing gate into another field. Stay with the left field edge. Exit via a kissing gate to a road. Turn right passing the drives of **Howick Grange** and **Red Stead Farm**. Cross a stone bridge over **Howick Burn** then go under a stone arch. Pass the entrance to **Howick Hall/Gardens**.

Howick Hall was built in 1782 by Sir Henry Grey. Its most famous resident was the second Earl Grey, the leader of the movement in 1831–32 which resulted in the passing of the Great Reform Act. He is commemorated on the top of a monument in Newcastle. He enlarged the Hall in 1812 and planted thousands of saplings. His son remembered family walks around the estate: 'It is difficult to exaggerate the beauty and variety of the sea coast and views that met you at every turn of the sea walk.' Seaview House was built as a base for the Grey family to go swimming.

❺ Where the car park drive turns left keep down a track, then along a left field edge. Go through a wide gate and on along the left field edge. Exit through a kissing gate and enter a field with a basalt cliff to the right. Cross diagonally towards the left end of the cliff. Cross a ladder stile then follow the same line past a couple of oak trees along the path signed to Craster. Go through a wide gate at

37

the end of the cliff then cross the field to go through a wicket gate at the field corner. Follow a grassy track along two right field edges to **Craster South Farm**. Keep on ahead to a tarmac lane and turn right down to a road. Cross this then go through a gate signed Craster and keep over a field towards another crag. Go through a kissing gate into the **Arnold Memorial Nature Reserve**. Stay with the main track through the little wood to exit near an information centre.

6 Cross the road and follow a sign to Dunstan Square through a wicket gate. Follow the path through another wicket gate and past a gorse-covered basalt ridge. Exit via a kissing gate. Turn left along the grassy track and go through a wide gate. Follow left field edges then exit through a wide gate onto the farm lane of **Dunstan Square**. Turn left and follow the lane past cottages to a junction with a road.

7 Turn right. When the road turns left take a very clear track off to the right (signposted to Dunstan Steads and Embleton). Follow this across the field to a corner where there is a bridge and a stile obscured by trees. Cross the bridge and stile and follow a path to the left along the edge of a wood. At the end of the field, go through a gate and keep on along the right side of a hedge. Pass a campsite on the left and cross a stile

at the end of the field. Bear right to cross a bridge onto a well-worn path through woods. Turn right and walk down to a gate and stile on the left. Cross the stile and go over the field to another stile and gate. Cross the stile and bear right down a dip, through a gate then turning left to go through another gate and over a bridge. Walk up to the road and turn left to walk up to a junction where you turn right and return to Embleton village.

In Embleton is the Old Manse (now a private residence) where a plaque commemorates the birth of famous crusading journalist William Thomas Stead who campaigned against child prostitution. He lost his life when the Titanic sank – an event which he imagined six years before in a short story called Futility. The Bishop of London and historian Mandell Creighton started his career here as a young vicar. The old vicarage has a fortified vicar's pele like that at Corbridge. Near the route is Dunstan Steads where was born the famous theologian Duns Scotus from whom the word 'dunce' is derived.

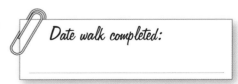

Date walk completed:

OLD BEWICK, HANGING CRAG, EGLINGHAM AND BLAWEARIE

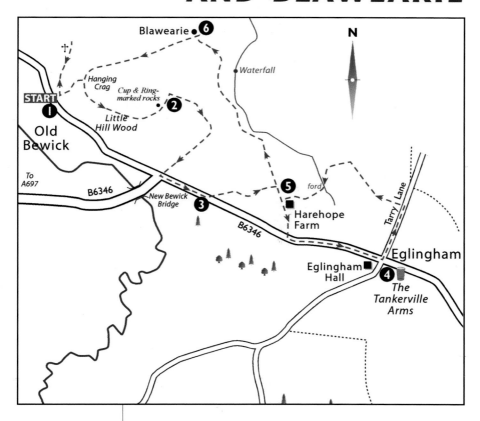

Distance:
10 miles

Starting Point:
Old Bewick.
GR 067215

Map: OS Explorer 332 Alnwick & Amble

How to get there: *Old Bewick is 6 miles south-east of Wooler and just off the B6346 linking the A697 and Alnwick. There is limited parking by the roadside at the small hamlet or beside the Norman church.*

ON THE PATH TO BLAWEARIE

*T*he bulk of this walk is across moorland although you have a stretch of road walking into Eglingham. This is an area of great tranquillity, especially at the abandoned, wind-blown farm of Blawearie and the little Norman church at Old Bewick. Appearances can be deceptive. This region was heavily populated in pre-Roman times and this is reflected in the high density of religious sites, burial mounds and cists, and the curious cup and ring markings on boulders. It was also rather more industrial than you might think. This is a classic Northumbrian walk with great views in all directions, but especially over the Cheviots.

The stone-floored **Tankerville Arms** in Eglingham dates from 1830 but is on the site of a much older inn. There is a smart comfortable bar with ceiling beams and an open fireplace. There is a spacious and stylish restaurant decorated with old prints and antique farm implements, and a beer garden with lovely views. The main beers are John Smith's, Hadrian & Border, Mordue's and Black Sheep. The staff are very friendly and accommodating. The same menu is available in both the restaurant and the bar at the same prices at both lunchtime and in the evening. Typical main courses are salmon on herb-baked tomatoes with melted Gruyère cheese, cod on a fennel potato bake, pork chunk with apple and onion ragout, and cannon of venison on chunky black pudding with roasted leeks. There is a good vegetarian menu. Specials are added on a daily basis. The mouth-watering range of reasonably priced desserts is worth exploring.

The Tankerville Arms is open from 12 noon to 11 pm Monday to Thursday, 12 noon to 12.30 am on Friday and Saturday and 12 noon to 10.30 pm on Sunday. Food is served from 12 noon to 9.30 pm.

Telephone: *01665 578444*; *www.tankervillearms.com*

 The Walk

1 At **Old Bewick** follow a footpath sign to Blawearie/Quarry House past houses and through a wide gate. Through the second, turn right and follow the stone wall and the fence on your right. Keep to a track below **Hanging Crag** and through a wide metal gate. The track bears left, skirting a hill, then climbs and passes a wood on the right. Go through a large area of rhododendrons. The path may not be very clear but keep the rhododendrons to the left. Beyond the rhododendrons and at the end of the hill, as you approach a wall, bear left steeply uphill meeting another track and reaching a wall corner. Beyond this is a small gate on the right. Here you could make a brief detour to the left along a path to a stile. Cross the stile and look at the cup and ring marks on the large boulder. There are others in this area.

2 Back at the gate go through and keep on ahead following the line of a fence on the right. The fence bends to the right but keep on ahead past a waymarked post on a clear bridleway which descends through thick heather and becomes sunken. It meanders down to rejoin the fence at the bottom of a hill by a gate. Go through this and follow a wide track through woods via a wide gate and onto a road. Walk down to a junction. Turn left and walk on to a public footpath sign on the left just before a dip in the road.

3 Turn left into woods. Follow a very faint path climbing up to the right then skirting a new plantation towards the main woodland path. Eventually you will hit a path along the top edge of the wood. Turn right and walk to the end of the wood. Beyond the trees bear left uphill to a wide wicket gate near the corner of a stone wall (with another wide gate just to the right). Go through and turn right and then left climbing up the track with the wall on the right. Go through a wide gate and follow the track as it bears right and descends through another gate. Turn right and go ahead through another gate and past **Harehope Farm**. Keep on to a public footpath sign on the left where you go through a gate and cross the paddock to a wicket gate in the opposite corner. Go through and bear right along the top of a ridge then descend with the path to a wide gate leading onto a road. Go through and turn left to walk carefully for ½ mile into **Eglingham** and to the **Tankerville Arms** passing **Eglingham Hall** and the rather grand **St Maurice's church**.

Eglingham (pronounced Eglingjum) is a small village built of honey-coloured sandstone. It stands in a sheltered situation and was described in an 1886 guidebook as enjoying 'a genial and invigorating air that gives increased health to the strong and imparts new life to those whose physical energies have temporarily deteriorated'. It was an estate village divided between two estates – the Tankervilles and the Ogles. There is still a Tankerville Arms and there was once an Ogle Arms. Do not be misled by the arcadian nature of the scenery because at one time there were collieries and limestone quarries in the area. The curiously-named Tarry Lane and Tarry House reflect the fact that there was a colliery at the top of the lovely tree-lined lane until 1910 and tar was a by-product.

4 Retrace your steps from the **Tankerville Arms** past the church to a crossroads. Turn right into **Tarry Lane** marked 'No Through Road'. Walk up this steep lane. At the end of the woods turn left at a sign for Harehope going through a wide gate onto the bridleway. Go through a gate and follow the grassy track as it bears right, then go through a gate and on towards a stone wall and a wicket gate. There is a plantation beyond the wall. Go through the gate. Then follow a grassy track, with the wall fairly near on the left side, as it bends right then left winding down through gorse to a gate. Go through then cross a footbridge. Walk up a slope with a wall on your left towards **Harehope Farm**. Go through two wide gates and on past cottages to a junction with another track.

HOLY TRINITY CHURCH AT OLD BEWICK

5 Turn right and go through a wide gate and up the farm track to a gate in the stone wall on the left. Go through then turn right and follow the wall on the right past a waymarked post. Stay with the path as it follows a fence on the right and then dips down to the left then to the right into the depression. Keep along the rutted track to cross a footbridge. Follow a path slightly left then towards the left end of a line of trees. Bear round the trees to reach a yellow waymarked wicket gate. Go through this and enter an open area. This can be boggy and the path is not clear. Note the small linn in the valley over on the right. Keep ahead with hills on both sides. Aim towards a lower slope in between where you will begin to see a path. A couple of isolated hawthorn trees mark a stone bridge. Cross this and go up to join a clear path. Now follow this in roughly the same direction past waymarked posts to arrive at the ruins of **Blawearie**.

Blawearie has been abandoned since the 1940s. It is difficult to see how anyone could live such an isolated life. The last inhabitants kept a cow but the nearest grazing is a mile away. Someone went to a lot of trouble to cultivate a garden in an outcrop of fell sandstone close by the cottage. The trees are the only ones on the whole moor, and must have been planted and tended with much care. There are even steps cut into the rock to provide access to the long-neglected shrubbery. The moor around here is full of pre-Roman and Romano-British remains, including a well-preserved hill fort on Bewick Hill, a burial tumulus which looks like a fallen sheep fold to the west of Blawearie and numerous cup and ring markings.

6 From **Blawearie**, with its air of *Wuthering Heights*, turn left (west) down a broad track past an ancient burial site on the right (not sheepfold ruins). Stay with the main track as it rises then descends past a kissing gate next to a wide gate and with **Hanging Crag** on the left. Keep on to another gate then another and go

through this following the track as it steepens. As you approach **Old Bewick** you come to another gate and a public footpath sign on the right marked **Bewick Folly**. Go through the gate then follow the fingerpost line over the field and making for the left end of a plantation. Descend to a hidden ladder stile. Cross this then turn left and walk, with the wall on the left, along the path to **Old Bewick**. To visit **Holy Trinity church**, turn right and cross a little stream by a stone slab footbridge.

Old Bewick's name derives from an OE word beo-wic meaning bee farm, although most of the moor was once wooded so there cannot have been much heather. The first lord of Old Bewick was called Arkle Moreal. He gained the title in 1093 for killing Malcolm, King of Scotland but then had it confiscated following his involvement in a rebellion two years later. The little church is a gem. Much of it is 11th or 12th-century. After damage by war and weather it was restored in 1867 but the original Norman style can still be discerned.

 Date walk completed:

SHILLMOOR, COPPER SNOUT, ALWINTON AND THE COQUET GORGE

LOOKING ACROSS THE COQUET TO BARROW SCAR

Distance:
10 miles

Map: OS Explorer OL 16 The Cheviot Hills

Starting Point:
Shillmoor.
GR 886076

How to get there: *Approach Shillmoor from the B6341 linking Rothbury and Otterburn. Follow a minor road through Alwinton and on to Shillmoor. You can park off the road at several points.*

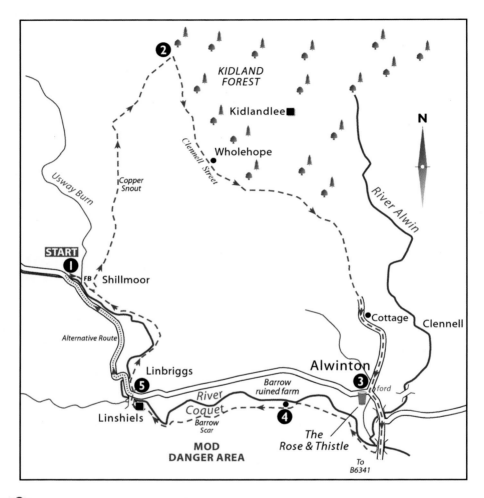

The **Rose and Thistle** in Alwinton is an unassuming single-storey stone building dating from the 13th century and was an alehouse long before it became a coaching inn in the 1750s. It is much bigger than it appears at first sight. There is a bar, a large lounge/restaurant area and a pleasant beer garden. You'll hear the genuine Northumbrian accent with its Hotspur 'r'. While here Sir Walter Scott penned much of *Rob Roy*, published in 1817. Beers include Farne Islands Bitter, Tetley's and Boddingtons. Bar meals are available at a reasonable price including home-baked steak pie and chips, gammon steak, scampi and chips, ham salad, cheese ploughman's, vegetable lasagne and chicken curry and rice. There is also a good range of sandwiches and children's meals.

The Rose and Thistle is open on Monday from 7 pm to 11 pm, Tuesday and Wednesday 12 noon to 3 pm and 7 pm to 11 pm, Thursday closed at lunchtime but open 7 pm to 11pm, Friday 12 noon to 3 pm and 7 pm to 11 pm, Saturday and Sunday 12 noon to 5 pm and 7 pm to 11 pm. Food is available from Tuesday to Saturday 12 noon to 2.30 pm and 7 pm to 9 pm and Sunday 12 noon to 2.30 pm.

Telephone: *01669 650226*; www.roseandthistlealwinton.com

---

*T*he views of the Cheviots to the north and the Simonside hills to the south are the great feature of this varied walk. A long gradual ascent to Copper Snout is followed by an even longer descent of the ancient Clennell Street, with lovely views, passing Kidland Forest for much of the way. The route accompanies the attractive rivers Coquet and Alwin for some time, and skirts the top of Barrow Scar. In between these is the narrow hillside path above the Coquet Gorge – or not, if you prefer to follow the quiet road below. Don't forget though, as if anyone would, to call in to the historic Rose and Thistle.

 The Walk

❶ Walk past the cottages and farmhouse of **Shillmoor**. Beyond a barn cross a bridge over the **Usway Burn** then a stile to follow a stony track as it winds and rises steadily. There are good views over Shillmoor and along the Coquet valley. It becomes more grassy and rises to a gate. Cross a stile and keep on. The track levels out, for now, and **Kidland Forest** is visible ahead. In the distance over to the left you can see **Windy Ghyle**. At a fork keep left. At another fork keep left and uphill. Stay with the pleasant grassy track and enjoy the Cheviot views with the little **Usway Burn** far below you. Keep on to a stile beside a wide gate. Cross this then turn right along the grassy path with a fence on the right. Cross another stile beside a gate then keep left with a fence on your left. Beyond a fence corner you finally reach a wide track along the forest edge. This is **Clennell Street**.

The Upper Coquet valley used to be a regular stop for Scottish drovers on their way to the markets at Hexham and Newcastle using a track called Clennell Street. It was also used by shepherds taking flocks to summer pastures and living in temporary shelters or shielings. At Alwinton, Clennell Street meets The Street which follows the Coquet, here emerging from the hills. The original settlement was probably near the isolated church of St Michael. Kidlandlee derives its name from the old lordship of Kidland in Upper Coquetdale which was Cydda's-land. Kidlandlee was built originally as a shooting lodge. This whole area was once a hunting ground.

2 Turn right and follow the track into the forest. At a fork keep left to reach another fork beside a marker post. Keep right through a wide gate to reach, through another gate, the ruins of the former **Wholehope youth hostel**. Keep on ahead to another stile to follow close alongside the forest edge with a fence on the right. Go through a gate and keep past a fence corner and sheepfolds. Continue up a slope on the grassy track. It descends into a wet peaty area then rises again, through another wide gate. Enjoy good views of the **Simonside hills**. Keep on down the track with a fence then a wall on the left. The **Clennell**

Hall Hotel and a caravan site are down on the left in the **Alwin valley**. At a waymarked post pass an isolated cottage and keep on alongside a fence to cross a ladder stile next to a wide gate. Keep on past a farm on the right and follow a metalled lane to arrive at the village green of **Alwinton** where you cross a footbridge over the **Hosedon Burn**. The **Rose and Thistle** is just ahead.

When this border area was under English control the pub was called the Rose, and when the Scots were dominant it became the Thistle. Only after the unification of the two kingdoms did it become the Rose and Thistle. This is the story locals tell, and it's worth listening to if only to hear the authentic Northumbrian accent. Coquetdale was once an area of 'debatable land' that was devastated by reiving for 300 years until 1603. It was in the English Middle March which, together with the East and West Marches, was in the charge of a Warden. The raiding families were virtually a law unto themselves – Armstrong, Hall, Forster, Carleton, Elliot, Noble and Storey, and others, were all famous 'riding' surnames. A report in 1541 said that it was impossible to get people to live here because of frequent Scottish raids and because the noise of a raid in one valley could not be heard in the

ALWINTON

***next so by the time help arrived
the cattle were gone!***

❸ From the **Rose and Thistle** turn
right and follow the road round to
the right, going south. Cross the
bridge over the **Alwin**, pass the
Netherton/Whittingham/Glanton
junction then **St Michael and All
Angels** church. Cross the bridge over
the **Coquet**. After that turn right
along a track signed to Linbriggs.
Follow this to the right between
barns to cross a stile beside a wide
gate with the noisy Coquet close by.
Keep on this narrow path, often wet
and overgrown. There is a prominent

bank on the left side. Pass the
junction of the **Coquet** and the
Barrow Burn. Keep on past a
solitary wooden post to cross a
footbridge over the **Barrow Burn**.
Turn left in a meadow and follow
the left edge across a stile and
on to **Barrow**.

*The waterway system here is
confusing. The bubbling Alwin runs
south from the Cheviot to join the
Coquet which rises further west
and traces an eastward course to
reach the sea at Amble.* Alwin
means white or clear water.
Coquet *means* red river (Celtic

49

cocc-wed). The Barrow Burn, which joins the Coquet here, is named after Barrow which will have been associated with some sort of burial mound of the local Celtic Ottadini tribe. The Hoseden Burn which runs through Alwinton seems to be a combination of hoh or hill or spur of land and denu which means valley.

4 Do not follow the obvious grassy track which leads into MOD property. Follow the line of the waymarker on the gate at Barrow to a marker post across to the right then follow a faint and variable path – the bracken can be dense – which takes you past three more marked posts to a wire fence above **Barrow Scar**. Turn left and follow the fence, ignoring tempting gaps. Descend on the path to cross a stile near a firing range notice. Follow a narrow path as it initially descends, through a new plantation, towards the burn. It bends left and winds round to a wooden gap stile. Beyond that, walk on to cross a ladder stile beside a wide gate. Cross over a field to the far corner beside **Linshiels** and exit over a stile. Go on through a wide gate then follow the farm track down to cross two bridges and turn right to walk up to the road.

5 Turn left. Beyond some barns is a public footpath sign. Follow the **Shillmoor** option and cross a patch of grass to cross a stile. Follow the fence on the left. The narrow path rises, levels then loses the fence. Contour the hill along this path. Be careful because in places there is a marked drop down to the Coquet below and the bracken can obscure the edge of the path. Pass a short narrow section of gorge beneath the path then a large group of trees. Eventually arrive at an awkward step stile and reach a wire fence which descends left towards sheepfolds, a ford and a clear wide track. That is not for you. Keep on ahead past the wire fence corner and follow the path to join a good track. Turn left and descend to a gate. Go through then cross a small stream and exit through another gate. Stay on the path and cross over a couple of tracks. Then just follow the obvious path ahead, initially with thick bracken on the left and then a wire fence. Keep on across a burn (narrow but sometimes difficult to cross) then continue on the path alongside a wall. Cross a stile and keep on to join a track and return to Shillmoor. *(NB: If you suffer from vertigo or are at all uncertain about the path described in point 5, the alternatives are to keep along the road to Shillmoor or follow the left bank of the Coquet.)*

Date walk completed:

WARKWORTH, THE RIVER ALN, LESBURY AND ALNMOUTH DUNES

ALNMOUTH SEEN FROM CHURCH HILL

Distance:
11½ miles

Starting Point:
The Hermitage Inn
in Warkworth.
GR 248062

Map: OS Explorer 332 Alnwick & Amble

How to get there: *Warkworth is 8 miles south-east of Alnwick on the A1068. There are several car parks and limited street parking in the village centre.*

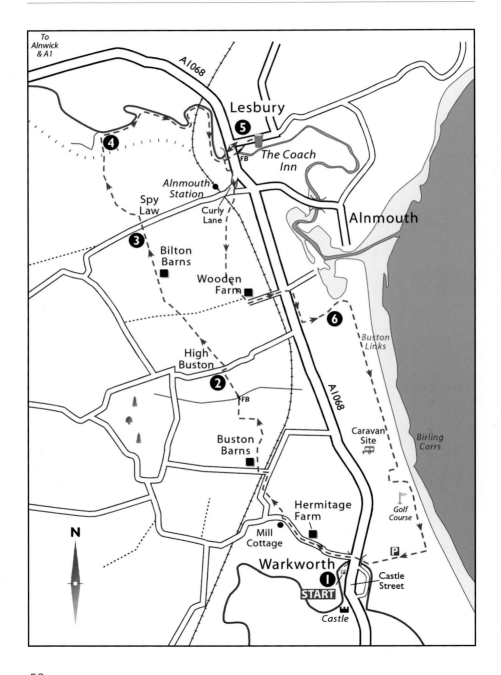

To Alnwick & A1

A1068

Lesbury

5

FB

The Coach Inn

Alnmouth Station

4

Spy Law

Curly Lane

3

Bilton Barns

Wooden Farm

Alnmouth

High Buston

2

FB

6

Buston Links

Buston Barns

Caravan Site

Birling Carrs

Hermitage Farm

Mill Cottage

Golf Course

P

N

Warkworth

1

START

Castle Street

Castle

From Warkworth, with its great medieval castle and fortified bridge, follow field edges, with views across the coastal stretch south of Alnmouth. Then descend into the Aln valley to follow the riverside to Lesbury, and the tempting Coach Inn. Most of the return route is over quiet fields then along a track past Alnmouth dunes and Warkworth beach and back to Warkworth.

The **Coach Inn** at Lesbury is an attractive pub dating from the 1750s. It is stone-built, beamed and has low ceilings. It is notable for its colourful displays of flower-filled baskets and tubs and the thatch-topped tables outside. There is an attractive lounge bar and a comfortable quiet snug. The dining room occupies the former village forge (the Coach Inn was originally called the Blacksmith's Arms). McEwan's, Black Sheep, Worthington and Stones beers are available. There is a good range of food with meat, fish and vegetarian dishes. Typically this might include home-made steak and ale pie, slow roasted Northumberland beef, asparagus omelette with cheese, maple-glazed gammon set on bubble and squeak, Rothbury Bangers with whole-grain mustard, Gressingham duck breast and border char-grilled salmon. There are also sandwiches and light bites and a good range of desserts.

The Coach Inn is open every day from 11 am to 11 pm. Food is available from 12 noon to 8.30 pm. Sunday lunch is served from 12 noon to 5 pm.

Telephone: *01665 830865*

Alnmouth has an excellent range of inns and restaurants but a visit would add about 1½ miles to your route.

 *The Walk*

❶ From the **Hermitage Inn** walk down **Castle Street** to cross the old medieval fortified bridge. Walk on up the main road for a few yards then left up the road to **Shilbottle**.

Follow the pavement past **Hermitage Farm** on the right and on to **Mill Cottage**. Opposite it cross a stile signed Buston Barns then follow the left field edge. Go through a gap in the tall hedge on the left into a big field. Turn right for a few yards then cross the field to the far side. Exit via a stile onto a quiet lane

53

by a signpost back to Mill Cottage. Turn right and along to a railway bridge. Cross the bridge to **Buston Barns**. Turn right between barns along a tarmac track between large fields. At a T-junction turn left and walk to a waymarked post by a telegraph pole. Turn right along the bridleway. Go through a wicket gate, cross a footbridge then follow the left edge of a new plantation to cross a path and go through a wicket gate. Now walk up fields to **High Buston** crossing two stiles en route. Exit onto a lane over a stile.

❷ Turn right towards **High Buston Hall** and at a signpost for Bilton (near a sign *Check Tap at Tanks*) turn left up a track. Go through a wide gate and follow the bridleway along the right field edge. Go through a wicket gate and in the field beyond bear half left towards buildings on the horizon. Go through a wicket gate in the hedge and on in roughly the same line to go through another wicket gate. Keep on across the next field to a wide gate then turn immediately left and through another wide gate. The right of way is diagonally across to the far corner. Then follow a track to **Bilton Barns** and a hedged drive.

❸ Cross the B1338 and go up a track to **Spy Law** (signed to Spy Law and Greenrigg). At two adjacent wide gates go across the stile between them and follow the path skirting the woodland edge. Exit down stone steps and keep on ahead across a field. Go through a wicket gate and down a steep bank to go through another wicket gate into a field. Follow the left edge to go through a kissing gate and onto a metalled lane at **Greenrigg**. Keep on down the lane across a bridge over a dismantled railway and to the meeting of the **Cawledge Burn** and the **River Aln**. Just before that turn right onto a gravel track with a high hedge on the right.

❹ Follow this pleasant riverside track with the little **Aln** the left. Bear round to the left at **Bilton Mill** and continue along the riverside. Go under the railway viaduct and keep on close to the riverside along a track which diminishes in size. At a fork in the track follow the right one which rises above the river (the older track on the left is eroded). This undulates on to a path junction where there are two benches. For **Lesbury** descend to the A1068 (the left fork) to cross the old bridge. Turn right down the main street for the **Coach Inn** in **Lesbury**.

It is claimed that Lesbury's name (Lechesbiri, 1190) means physician's or leeche's manor. Lesbury church is an ancient foundation dedicated to St Mary. In the churchyard are the graves of the 7th Duke of Northumberland and his family.

For some years after 1806 residents of Alnmouth were buried here because Alnmouth church and its burial ground were washed away in a flood. Lesbury House was formerly the dower house of widows of the dukes of Northumberland.

5 To continue, return to the benches at the hill-top junction and take the other fork. At a path T-junction near a facing hedge turn left and descend through a kissing gate onto a tarmac path. Turn right and walk to a road junction. Turn right and walk up **Curly Lane** through a housing estate. At a sharp right bend cross the road to follow a tarmac path (near a residents' car park) and exit onto the B1338 via a fence gap. Cross the road and go through a wicket gate signed Wooden Farm. Descend the bank, then once through a kissing gate follow the right field edge. Go through a wide gate and under the railway bridge. Bear half left across a field. Go through a wide gate and follow the right field edge. At a facing fence and small enclosure go through the hurdle and keep on to exit via a wicket gate into a field to continue with the right edge to **Wooden Farm**. Turn right through a couple of wide gates. At a track junction turn

THE IMPOSING WARKWORTH CASTLE

left through a wide gate and at barns turn right along a metalled lane. Follow this to **Wooden Gate**. Cross the railway line then the main road to a junction at a sign to Waterside House. Turn right and follow a cycleway separated from the busy road by a hedge. At a junction with a track turn left down the public bridleway to **Buston Links**. At a sign to Birling Carrs/Coastal Path turn right and follow a wide track to a gate.

The prominent sandy hill on the left is Church Hill. On Christmas Day in 1806 the river, which flowed in a loop round the south side, changed its course as a result of a huge storm. It broke through into a more direct route to the sea and washed away the remains of the old Saxon church. The harbour was no longer viable. Overnight

Alnmouth lost its significance as a corn port. However, the railway encouraged the development of tourism. By 1852 one local historian wrote: 'In the summer season the village is filled with the inhabitants of Alnwick and District, who resort to it for sea bathing. The sands are beautifully firm and the adjoining grassy links smooth as velvet carpet in the sunshine of a hot summer's day – most enjoyable.' The cross on Church Hill marks the site of the former church and also of the Synod of Twyford in AD 684 when St Cuthbert was persuaded to become Abbot of Lindisfarne.

6 You can walk along the beach if it is safe to do so. Otherwise follow the dunes track. Go through the gate and follow the track which narrows, rises and runs alongside a stone wall on the right. Descend to cross a footbridge and enter the caravan site near the beach (where you exit from the beach if you took that route). Keep ahead through the caravan site. You see **Birling Carrs** and **Amble Beach** to the left. Follow the left edge of **Warkworth Golf Course**. The track bends right then left across the course. Through a gate turn left and descend into a gully beneath a wooden bridge. At a beach lifebuoy point turn right and follow the sandy path beneath the dunes then along the left edge of the golf course. Exit via a gap in the fence at a signpost

to Warkworth/Warkworth Beach. Turn right to **Warkworth** up a track. This becomes a path and crosses the access road to a car park. Cross a caravan park drive then follow the right field edge. Exit onto a minor road and turn left along the main road back into **Warkworth**.

This fine example of a medieval planned town was laid out near the lowest crossing of the Coquet. Tomlinson described Warkworth as 'seated on a steep declivity, almost encircled by the lovely Coquet …'. The skyline is dominated by the castle. In 1332 Warkworth was taken over by the Percy family who were responsible for putting Henry IV on the throne but they then rebelled and were defeated. Three scenes in Shakespeare's Henry IV are set in 'this worm-eaten hold of ragged stone'. The Norman church of St Lawrence was once the site of a massacre of 300 people when Scottish invaders burnt it. In 1715 the Jacobites proclaimed the Old Pretender as king in Warkworth. The fortified bridge (1379) is unusual in northern England. The new bridge was built in 1965.

Date walk completed:

SIMONSIDE, GREAT TOSSON, ROTHBURY AND THE FOREST BURN

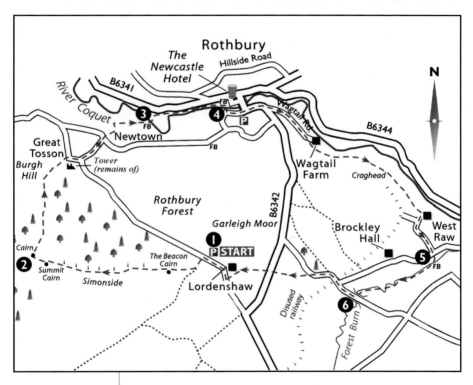

Distance:
12 miles

Starting Point:
Great Tosson
Forestry
Commission car
park (free).
GR 053987

Maps: OS Explorer OL 42 Kielder Water & Forest and
OS Explorer 325 Morpeth & Blyth

How to get there: *Great Tosson car park is 2 miles south
of Rothbury on a minor road west of the B6342.*

ON THE SUMMIT OF SIMONSIDE

*C*limb one of the iconic hills of Northumberland whose strange profile dominates the horizon in this area and which pre-Roman people regarded as a site of great religious significance. Walk along the top and enjoy excellent views. Return along a dismantled railway, across moorland, through woodland, along the twisting Forest Burn and along the edge of the River Coquet.

The **Newcastle Hotel** stands in the centre of Rothbury. It is Edwardian in origin with a coloured glass portico, dark wood and brass bar fittings and coloured glass screens. There is a public bar and a lounge bar attached to a small restaurant. There are always three real ales on offer and guest ales are constantly being added. The main beers are Worthington, Tetley's, Newcastle Exhibition, Foster's and John Smith's. Meals are cooked from fresh ingredients which are sourced locally as far as possible. There is a full range of seafood and fish dishes, meat dishes, chicken and lasagne.

Vegetarian food includes stuffed peppers, peppered vegetables and corn on the cob. There is also a good range of salads. The staff are very friendly and obliging.

The Newcastle Hotel is open daily from 11 am to 12 pm Monday to Thursday and Sunday, and 11 am to 1 am on Friday and Saturday. Food is served from 12 noon to 9 pm on Friday, Saturday and Sunday, and on Monday to Thursday 12 noon to 3 pm and 6 pm to 9 pm, with a more restricted menu from 3 pm to 6 pm.

Telephone: *01669 620334*

 The Walk

1 From **Great Tosson** car park cross the road following the sign to Spylaw and Coquet Cairn and follow the stone slab path. At a waymarked post turn right. Pass a large cairn then cross a facing fence using a ladder stile. Ascend stone steps and keep on ahead, ignoring a bridleway leading to the right, past another cairn and impressive weathered rock outcrops. Up more steps continue along the path to the **Simonside** summit cairn on a rocky knoll. To continue keep to the left, winding round outcrops onto a boggy plateau. Cross this on stone slabs. Keep to the left of another cairn. At a fork go right and begin your careful descent down a steep and rocky way. Arriving at the main forest track turn left. After a few yards turn right at a marker post to follow a narrow path.

Simonside is a Special Area of Conservation. It is 1,409 ft high. The plants and animals are of importance at a European level. The area is notable for the extent of blanket bog, a rare habitat, and because it has some of the remaining heather moorland left in the world. Simonside is also very rich in archaeological sites. The 'Sacred Mountain' is littered with burial mounds dating back 4,000 years. It is also, apparently, the home of mischievous elves which lure people over bogs or into caves! The name is said to be derived from Sigemund's Seat or settlement. In 1279 the name was Simunessette.

2 Follow the difficult path through dense heather into woods. Cross one forest track and keep on. At another track turn right then left through a wicket gate. Follow a grassy path bending right. Cross a stile by a wide gate in a facing fence and keep on.

At a fork keep right with the wall/fence on your right. Cross a permissive path to **Tosson Burgh Hill Fort** to descend. Go through a kissing gate then exit onto a track via a stile by a wide gate. Turn right past farm buildings and join a lane at **Great Tosson**. Keep ahead at a junction passing **Tosson Tower** on the right. Continue along the metalled lane. At a fork keep left, descending to another junction near **Newtown**. Turn left then right at another junction for **Tosson Mill**. At **Weaver's Cottage** follow a right bending track to arrive at a footbridge over the **Coquet**.

Tosson Tower was a home of the Ogles. It dates back to the 15th century although relatively little is left. In 1715 John Warburton wrote 'Great Tosson: a small village south of ye river Coquet, in which is ye remains of an old pile'. This sort of fortified house was very necessary in an area such as Coquetdale which was open to raiding by the Scots and the reivers of Tynedale and Redesdale. In 1549 a range of warning beacons was established in the county, and in 1553 a system of 'watch and ward' was established in every township and community.

NEWCASTLE HOTEL IN THE CENTRE OF ROTHBURY

When the watch raised the alarm by blowing horns and shouting, every able man had to follow on pain of death.

3 Across the bridge turn right through a kissing gate following the sign to Rothbury bearing half right across a field. Cross a footbridge in the far corner then keep on. At a path junction turn right. Keep on across another footbridge then keep on with the Coquet on the right. Go through a wicket gate then past the end of a wide bridge. Pass a picnic site on the left and keep on to arrive at a play area and a footbridge at **Rothbury** linking to the main town car park. Turn left here and walk to the village centre, and the **Newcastle Hotel**.

Rothbury is often called the capital of Coquetdale. It is the wooded, heather-clad hills which give it a distinctive setting and which have made it such a popular tourist resort. A railway branch line from Scots Gap was opened in 1870 and put Rothbury on the map. The line ran through attractive countryside and the gentle run down wooded slopes to Rothbury was considered quite spectacular. A name associated with Rothbury is William George, first Lord Armstrong of Cragside. He was an inventor, scientist and industrialist who pioneered the use of hydraulic power. He built the

mock-Gothic Cragside Hall on the edge of Rothbury using the great fortune that resulted from his activities, especially the armaments trade.

4 To continue, go to the car park. Turn left onto the road. Walk past the end of the road bridge and up to a Y-junction. Turn left along **Wagtail Road** (signed St Oswald's Way as well). The lane descends to an old railway line at **Wagtail Farm**. Turn right along the line between bridge abutments and through a gate. Follow the track, through more gates, then cross a step stile on the left. Bear half right to pass in front of **Craghead**. Follow the track over a culverted stream and through a gate. Cross the next field and go through another gate. Keep on with a fence on the right and through another gate. Cross the middle of the next field and go through another gate. Follow the edge of the next field to another gate. Follow a hedged track to **West Raw Farm**. At the farm take a right fork to go through a wide gate then turn right along the drive to a lane. Walk left past a pond and **Butterknowles Farm** then **East Raw** to a junction (signed Brinkburn Station). From here you can either turn right and walk up the quiet lane to reach point 6 – or follow the **Forest Burn**.

5 Cross over to go through a wicket gate (signed The Lee and Embleton

Terrace). Veer slightly left across the field and cross a step stile into woodland. Turn right along the path to meet the **Forest Burn**. Continue down to the left to cross a footbridge. The path is waymarked. Past the bridge follow the right marker. The path winds round to the right and crosses a side stream. Continue on to cross a step stile then cross a small meadow. Keep on, going through a wicket gate to rejoin the path alongside the burn. Turn down left across a small side stream then along a narrow clearing where there is no obvious path. At the end the path re-enters the woods. Cross the first meander of the burn then a second. Keep ahead to cross again, and through a clearing to cross again and join a clear path turning left. Cross again and keep on alongside the burn to the next crossing. Walk ahead for a few yards to cross for the last time. Beyond a marker post cross a stile into a meadow and keep on to a gate. Go through this to reach a road, ford and bridge.

6 Turn right passing a road junction on the right signed Longframlington and Pauperhaugh (where the alternative route from point 5 joins). Cross a stone bridge. Pass a bridleway sign on the left. Woodland appears along on your right. Keep on and go through a gate on the left signed Rothbury Road. There is no clear path. Aim for the right flank of **Simonside**. Cross a couple of old field boundaries and arrive at a fence. Cross a step stile and keep on over the small field to exit onto the B6342 by another step stile (signed back to Lee Siding). Cross the road and go over a stile next to a gate signed Lordenshaw. Keep ahead onto an old cart track. Go through a gate then cross a little stream on stone slabs. Pass in front of **Lordenshaw Farm** and go through two gates to join the road. Turn right and return to the car park.

If you take the clear grassy path from the north-west corner of the car park onto Garleigh Moor, you can look at a large sandstone rock covered in strange Bronze Age cup and ring markings. Close by are a number of burial grounds, remains of a fortified camp and the remains of an avenue of standing stones. From here you can see Rothbury clearly.

 Date walk completed:

MITFORD, THE DYKE NEUK AND THE LOWER WANSBECK VALLEY

MITFORD CASTLE'S CIRCULAR KEEP

Distance:
10 miles

Starting Point:
Mitford. Near the
church of St Mary
Magdalene,
GR 169856, or at
the Plough Inn.
GR 173860

Map: OS Explorer 325 Morpeth & Blyth

How to get there: *Mitford is 2 miles west of Morpeth on the B6343. There is limited roadside parking near the church. Alternatively, and if agreed by the manager, use the car park of the Plough.*

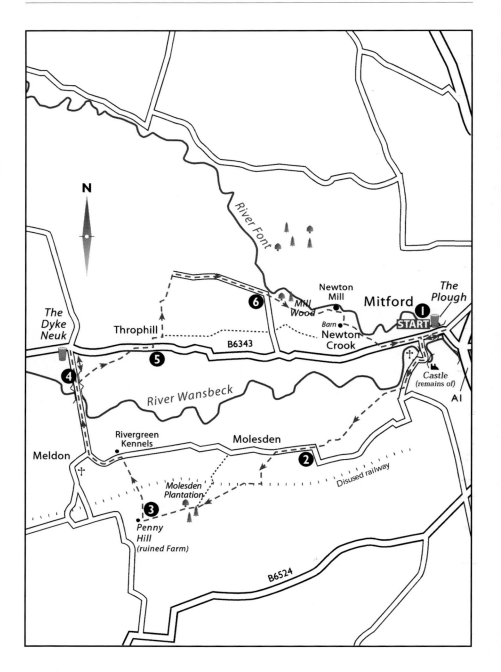

N

River Font

The Plough

Newton Mill

Mitford

START **1**

6

Mill Wood

The Dyke Neuk

Throphill

Barn

Newton Crook

B6343

Castle (remains of)

5

A1

4

River Wansbeck

Rivergreen Kennels

Molesden

Meldon

2

Disused railway

Molesden Plantation

3

Penny Hill (ruined Farm)

B6524

You will probably not encounter many walkers and will appreciate the peace and quiet of this lower Wansbeck area even though bustling Morpeth is not far away. At one end is Mitford with its very fine church and the remains of a once-prominent castle. At the other there is the oddly-named Dyke Neuk. In between much of the walk is along field edges, through woodland fringes and on quiet lanes. There are pleasant views over the valley on the outward stretch then across the lovely valley of the Font as you return to Mitford. There are no gradients of any note but there is the frightening witch, Meg of Meldon.

The **Dyke Neuk** at Meldonpark Corner is an imposing, rambling, old coaching inn with an intriguing name. It is large, open plan, beamed and has an open fireplace. There is a pleasant beer garden. Real ales on offer include Wylam's Northern Kite and Hadrian & Border Brewery's Old Kiln, along with John Smith's and Worthington. There are wide-ranging bar and restaurant menus on offer, mostly standard dishes, reasonably priced, but very substantial helpings. Try the venison sausage and mash or the 14 oz gammon steak and chips for instance, but remember you have several more miles ahead of you! There is a children's menu, and vegetarian dishes, sandwiches and jacket potatoes are available.

The Dyke Neuk bar is open from 12 noon to 11 pm on weekdays, 12 noon to 12 midnight on Friday and Saturday and 12 noon to 10.30 pm on Sunday. Food is served between 12 noon and 9 pm weekdays and 12 noon to 6 pm on Sunday.

Telephone: *01670 772662*

There is also the Plough Inn in Mitford if you choose to start at the Dyke Neuk (point 4). **Telephone:** *01670 512587*

The Walk

1 If you have parked at the **Plough Inn**, turn right and walk uphill along the B6343, then turn left downhill along the minor road passing **Snuff Mill** on the left then cross a bridge and pass **Mitford Castle** on the left and the **church of St Mary Magdalene** on the right. Keep on with the **Wansbeck** below you on the right. At a public footpath sign on the right go through a kissing gate and follow the right edge of the field. Cross a small footbridge and go through a wicket gate then follow the right edge of this next field round to cross two stiles with a small footbridge between them. Keep on now across a series of five more fields. Keep along the right edge of the next field initially then bear half left at a fence corner to cross the next stile. Keep half left across the next field then cross a footbridge and go over the track to cross a stile into the next field. Now follow the left edge (on the right side of the hedge) to cross another stile. Follow the right edge round to cross another stile, then a footbridge and another stile. Then follow the left edge of a field to exit finally onto a road.

The origin of the River Wansbeck's name is unclear. It has been traced to the spelling Wenspic in 1137 and it may be derived from the Old English waegn-spic which would mean a wagon and brushwood causeway. Most river names predate the Anglo-Saxons though and their origins and meaning are difficult to trace. Incidentally, Morpeth may be innocently derived from words meaning the path across the moor. However, the name in 1200 was Morthpath, which could mean murder path!

2 Keep straight ahead to **Molesden** passing a bridleway sign to Penny Hill/West Edington. At a footpath sign to Penny Hill/West Edington (just past a big barn on the left) turn left and enter a field through a gate, then follow the left edge. Go through a field gate then cross a dismantled railway and cross a stile into a field. Turn right and follow the right field edge (parallel to the railway) to a ladder stile. Cross this into the next field. Now the right of way is along the left edge but you may find that there is just a wooden section rather than a proper stile in the new facing fence. Just turn right and follow the fence to a wide gate. Go through, turn left then walk diagonally on a bridleway route to the far right corner of the field where you can enter the next field through a fence by the edge of the **Molesden Plantation** (just a few yards from a stile which is on the line of the right of way) and walk on to a gate into the woods which you now enter. Go through and exit via another wicket gate into a field. Keep on ahead across the field, then through another wide gate (bridleway marked) and follow the right edge through another wide gate and then on towards **Penny Hill Farm** along the right field edge.

3 Just before the farm turn right to cross a ladder stile. Now follow an obvious raised grassy track across a field to go through a wide gate. Keep on ahead with woods to your right. Go through a gate, cross the old railway line and continue through another gate to cross a field in the same northerly direction. Cross a stile then keep on to a road beside the **Rivergreen Kennels** via a gate (noting that all dead stock must be left before 1.00 pm!). Turn left and follow the road

THE DYKE NEUK PUB

as it bends to the right. At a road junction keep on ahead following the sign for Morpeth/Mitford/Hartburn. This is a quiet road in an attractive setting. Follow it as it dips down to the **Wansbeck** and crosses two bridges. Carry on up the lane to the **Dyke Neuk** at **Meldonpark Corner** if you so desire, then you will need to retrace your steps to the second bridge to continue the walk.

The little hamlet of Dyke Neuk (or Meldon Dyke Neuk) is close to Meldon with its little Early English church. This area is notorious for the mysterious doings of the witch Margaret 'Meg of Meldon', wife of Sir William Fenwick of Wallington and daughter of a Newcastle moneylender. An avaricious and miserly woman she was detested by local people. Stories were told of her hiding great treasures in various places which were haunted by her spirit after she died. It was also claimed that she had the ability to change into the form of a great black dog which was frequently seen to cross Meldon Bridge. The name Dyke Neuk will be derived from the fact that there was an embankment with a marked corner here.

4 The route continues from a lay-by where you go down a track to a footbridge and stile. Cross these into a field then keep on half left to follow the right side of a wood. Go through a gate and keep ahead. Now follow the right side of the old field boundary on your left and then a plantation fence on your right. At the end of the fence and hawthorns bear half left across the field to a gate to exit onto the B6343 over a stile. Now turn right and walk along this to **Throphill**.

5 At a bridleway sign on the left to East Thornton and Nunriding, turn up a lane past cottages and houses then on to a T-junction with a track. Turn right and follow a sign ahead to Nunriding Hall/Stanton Mill. Follow as it bends sharp left. Keep on up this green lane and at the end where there is a T-junction at a field edge turn right and follow the right field edge round to exit onto a very quiet minor road. Now follow this road, enjoying pleasant views and looking over the noisy little **Font Burn** which joins you from the left.

6 Where the road bends sharp right keep on ahead at a sign for Mitford and go through a gate onto a path. Keep on to cross a stile by a wide gate and carry on along the right field edge. Now the route continues into a pleasant woodland fringe and then descends to join the Font. This is a lovely stretch. At **Newton Mill** cross a stile by a gate then keep on ahead along the right side of the fence and go through a couple of wicket gates to join a lane. Walk up the bank and when you reach a ruinous barn turn left just beyond it along the right side of a fence and hedge. Keep on through a patch of woodland and through a

metal gate beside **Newton Crook**. Then bear half right over a field to cross a ladder stile and keep on half right to exit onto a road across a stile (signed back to Coal House) opposite the **Mitford Cricket Ground**. Now turn left and walk along the pavement back into **Mitford** and down to the **Plough Inn**.

Mitford stands near the junction of the River Font and the Wansbeck. The latter almost encircles Mitford Hall which was designed by John Dobson in 1828. Mitford Castle was built in 1118 by William Bertram, founder of Brinkburn Priory. It was destroyed in 1318 by Alexander III of Scotland. The circular keep on its artificial mound is still impressive but little remains of the curtain walls. The very grand church of St Mary Magdalene is mostly Victorian-restored but does have a number of Norman and medieval features, including the South Arcade. One building was once a snuff mill and before that a flannel factory, so farming was by no means the only enterprise. The settlement is named after the famous old Northumbrian Mitford family.

Date walk completed:

REDESMOUTH, BIRTLEY, WARK AND COUNTESS PARK

A FISHERMAN'S HUT BY THE NORTH TYNE

Distance:
11 miles

Starting Point:
Redesmouth.
GR 866822

Maps: OS Explorer OL 42 Kielder Water & Forest and OS Explorer OL 43 Hadrian's Wall

How to get there: *Redesmouth is 2 miles south-east of Bellingham on a minor road off the B6320. There is some roadside parking.*

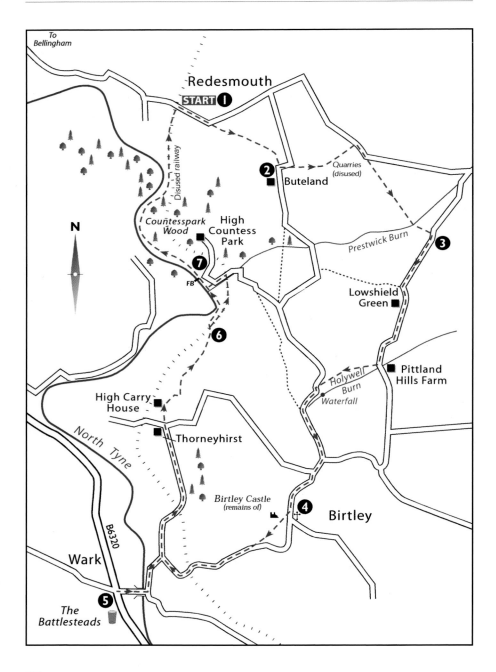

*M*ost of this walk is over rolling pasture but there is also a lovely woodland section through Countess Park. There are a couple of road sections but they are along quiet lanes with pleasant views. Make a brief excursion to Wark, once a home of the court of the king of Scotland, and pay a visit to the Battlesteads inn. Ponder over the meaning of some of the local place names on the way. Who on earth was Goodwife Hot for instance? And marvel at the agility of the Devil as he bounded across the attractive countryside of the valley of the North Tyne to his death!

The **Battlesteads** at Wark was originally built as a farmstead in 1747. This family-run inn and restaurant near the banks of the North Tyne features an open fireplace, a sunny walled garden, excellent bar meals and à la carte menus using fresh, local produce. There is a good choice of wines and a wide range of cask and bottle-conditioned beers from local micro-breweries. Main beers are Black Sheep, Wylam, Nel's Best, Durham Brewery and John Smith's. Meals, snacks and sandwiches are available throughout the day. Children's portions of main menu dishes are available. Local ingredients are used. The owners have their own flock of sheep at Belsay, hence the Northumbrian lamb steak. Other temptations are warm salad of wild rabbit, black pudding and apple, poached salmon niçoise, and twice-baked goats cheese soufflé with chives and roasted ham. Those sheep appear again on the evening menu with lamb cutlets, pan fried with leek roulade, minted new potatoes and rosemary gravy, alongside dressed crab and king prawn salad from North Shields Fish Quay, and caramelised wild mushroom tart served with roasted baby tomatoes and black-peppered sauté potatoes. There are also specials which change weekly.

The Battlesteads is open from 11 am to 11 pm. Lunch is served from 12 noon to 3 pm and dinner is served between 7 pm and 9.30 pm. Breakfast is available to non-residents from 7.30 am to 9.30 am.

Telephone: *01434 230209*; www.battlesteads.com

The Walk

❶ From **Redesmouth**, walk south-east along the road. Where it turns left cross a ladder stile signed Buteland, then follow roughly the same line over the field to cross a stile beyond a small stream. Head up to a wicket gate and through that follow the wall on your right. Ignore the ladder stile and a couple of gates on the right. Continue to go through a gate at the right field corner. There are good views behind you of **Bellingham** and the **North Tyne valley**. Bear right to join a road at **Buteland** near a sign to Redesmouth.

2 Turn left down to the metal gate in the wall corner. Follow the line of the footpath sign past old quarry workings. Exit via a gate onto a road. Turn right and follow this for a few hundred yards until it turns left and here you cross a ladder stile and walk on alongside a wall on the right, passing a large copse on the left and descending into the valley of the little **Prestwick Burn**. At a wall intersection cross the burn, go through a gate and then follow the wall up a slope to join a quiet, unfenced road.

3 Turn right along the road. Pass **Lowshield Green Farm**, go through a road gate and keep on towards **Pittland Hills Farm**. Just before the farm go through a gate on the right by a footpath and bridleway sign. Follow the wall on the right. Where the wall turns sharp right just keep on the same line, parallel to the **Holywell Burn valley** on the left, passing a marker post and making

for the left end of a plantation. Join a road here and turn left and pass the point where the **Holywell Burn** spills into a dene, the site of the Holy Well, and the large stone which is the subject of a legend about the Devil. From here either follow the road into **Birtley** or follow the line of the footpath sign to Birtley on the left – this takes you along an ill-defined grassy path, parallel to the road then by a stone wall on the right and over a ladder stile back onto the road and into **Birtley**.

St Giles' church in Birtley is 19th-century apart from its Norman chancel arch. In the vicarage garden there is a ruined tower standing 8 or 10 ft high facing the slope down to the valley. It was built in 1611 and may have been the vicar's pele. This area is full of earthworks and barrows, pre-Roman and Romano-British. The most curiously named is Goodwife Hot. The hot or holt probably means hill or clump of trees, and Goodwife may have been a term for the Goddess of Fertility. Above the Holy Well is the Devil's Stone which is 12 ft high. On the top of this are marks which resemble the cloven hoofmarks of the Devil. It is claimed that he tried to jump across the North Tyne from here to Lee Hall, and fell into Leap Crag Pool where he drowned. If true, this would pose problems for theologians worldwide!

④ In **Birtley**, walk down to **St Giles' church**. Opposite the church follow a signposted path past 'Birtley Castle' to cross a stile into a field which you cross diagonally to the bottom left corner. Cross a stile and a plank across a burn. This is followed by a short, steep rise by the wood side – then downhill on the other side, bearing left to a gate and onto the road to **Wark**. Turn right and walk to **Wark**, crossing the iron bridge over the **North Tyne**. To reach the **Battlesteads pub** walk up **Main Street** and turn left along the B6320.

THE DEVIL'S STONE

For a period in the 12th century, Tynedale was ruled by the kings of Scotland who held court at Wark where there was once a motte and bailey castle. Being part of the estate of the Earl of Derwentwater, who was executed for his part in the 1715 Jacobite rising, the parish was forfeited to the Crown and was passed on to Greenwich Hospital which put in naval chaplains as rectors. Wark's agricultural origins are symbolised by the Grey Bull Inn and Black Bull Inn which coexist close to each other. The village stands on the edge of the enormous Wark Forest, the largest wooded area in the Northumberland National Park

and home to roe deer and red squirrels.

⑤ To resume your walk re-cross **Wark Bridge** and turn left. The road bends right and rises. At a sign to Low Carry House, turn left to walk along a very pleasant, largely unfenced lane, with good views of Wark and the valley of the North Tyne. Go through a wide gate across the road and keep on past **Thorneyhirst Cottage** on the left. Just past the cottage, as the road bends to the left, cross over onto a rough track to go through a gate and keep on with a cottage on the right then through another gate to the ruins of **High Carry House**. Walk to the right of the ruins to go through a gate where you turn left to cross a ladder stile. Turn right and follow the stone wall and fence on the right crossing a dip. From here turn left and bear left to cross rough pasture towards the **North Tyne** which you can see now. Go through a small wicket gate and down the steps to the old railway.

6 Here you have a choice. You can follow the river edge, as long as the water is not high, or you can turn right along the railway. For the former go up the steps, cross a stile then bear right to cross a stile at the bottom corner of the field. The path follows the river. It is very rough and difficult and you need to be well shod, careful and nimble. Exit this wooded section across a stile into a meadow. Follow the river edge, crossing a small footbridge across a side stream to reach a road. If the little bridge is still under repair, you can simply bear right on a permissive footpath to join the road. If you chose to walk along the railway track, you would join the same lane near **Heugh**. Then turn left down the lane. Before you is an impressive house.

7 Walk on beneath the house to your right and into **Countesspark Wood**. The path through this lovely mixed woodland is picturesque and easy. Pass a rustic fishing lodge/boathouse. Watch out for heron. The views of the river through tall fringing conifers are lovely. The track reduces to a path and bears up to the right to steps and a ladder stile which takes you onto the old railway. Turn left and walk between the former platforms to the left of the old signal box, passing a restored waiting room/office on the right. You can see old engine sheds ahead of you. At the end of the platform turn up to the right and bear half left across the field to exit at the far left corner (NB – the right of way has been diverted here). Join a lane and walk along to the left to meet the road at **Redesmouth**.

'Sweet Redesdale' with its 'winding glens' starts at Redesmouth. Appearances can be deceptive. The Rede valley was once one of the most notorious haunts of the border moss-troopers who emerged from their wilderness to ravage the land between the Coquet and Wansbeck, stealing cattle and extorting 'blackmail'. The law was not easily applied because witnesses and informers feared becoming victims of clan vendetta and revenge. So bad was the reputation of Redesdale men that in 1564 the Merchant Adventurers of Newcastle passed a rule to prohibit any merchant from taking on a person from Redesdale or Tynedale as an apprentice.

Date walk completed:

BOLAM, SHAFTOE CRAGS, SHORTFLATT TOWER AND BELSAY

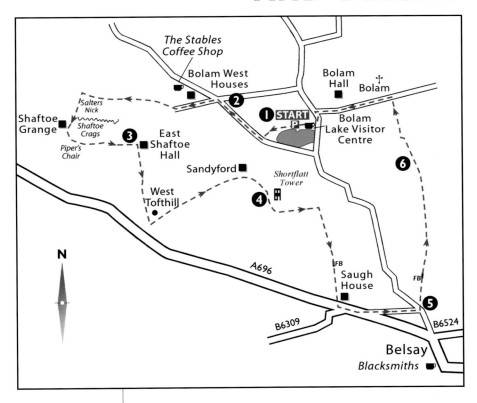

Distance:
11½ miles

Starting Point:
Bolam Lake
Visitor Centre.
GR 084821

Maps: OS Explorer OL 42 Kielder Water & Forest and OS Explorer 316 Newcastle upon Tyne

How to get there: *Bolam Lake is 8 miles north-west of Ponteland just off the A696. From the north end of Belsay follow the road sign to Scots Gap and Bolam Lake Country Park. Park in the Boathouse Wood car park (fee paying) near the visitor centre.*

THE CANYON KNOWN AS SALTERS NICK

A Saxon church, a scenic swan lake, a crenellated castle, a Buddhist monastery and a feisty 17th-century dame condemned never to be buried in consecrated ground. These are all features of this walk. You can also visit the Tuscan-style estate village of Belsay, walk along a stretch of mock Roman road, and come close to the line of the Devil's Causeway which was a real one. There are no inns on the route. Instead you have a choice of three excellent coffee shops, and potential picnic spots round every corner.

The **Stable Coffee Shop** at Bolam West Houses is open all year Friday to Monday from 10.30 am to 4.30 pm. The **Bolam Lake Visitor Centre Café** is open from Easter to November, 10.30 am to 4.30 pm weekends, Bank Holidays and school holidays. From December to Easter it is open from 12 noon to 3.30 pm at weekends and during school holidays. The

Blacksmith's in Belsay (near the entrance to Belsay Hall) is open every day but Monday from 10 am to 5 pm.

▌**Telephone:** The Stable *01661 881244;* Bolam Lake Visitor Centre *01661 881234;* The Blacksmith's *01661 881024*

 The Walk

❶ From **Bolam Lake Visitor Centre** walk down to the lake. Turn right to follow the path which circles the lake. Through the clearing called the **Pheasant Field** progress onto duck boarding which takes you into the **West Wood Car Park**. Cross over this and follow the footpath through coniferous trees and over a wider track. You walk virtually parallel to the road. Cross several plank bridges. Exit onto the road near a sign to Harnham and turn right. The road is quiet but traffic is fast.

In 1816 work began on creating this landscape by excavating the lake from the former 'splashy land'. The dam and the surrounding woodland were designed by John Dobson who went on to be architect for Central Station and most of Grey Street in Newcastle. During the Second World War, Land Army Girls and Italian POWs felled woodland here. It has become a popular countryside resort for Tynesiders. In 1972 the lake and

woodland were bought by the County Council who created the country park. The woodlands contain a variety of animal and plant species. There are red squirrels, stoats, weasels, foxes and roe deer. On the lake there are mute swans, tufted duck, mallard, coots and moorhens.

❷ At a junction at **Bolam West Houses** turn left along a public footpath to **Shaftoe Crags** along a rocky track with lime trees on the right. Keep on to a grassy area where you follow a wall on the right, with masses of gorse on the other side and lovely views across to the **Simonside hills**. Go through a gate and then keep on. Go down an unusual dry canyon known as the **Salters Nick**. At the end of this follow the wall on your right round to the left (or cut across half left – but this can be very muddy and wet) and follow the path round past **Shaftoe Grange**. Turn left when the path joins a wide track. Ignore paths to the left (which would take you up to the trig point and excellent panoramic views). Over to the right you can see the unusual rock formation known as the

Piper's Chair which you may care to visit. Beneath it is a cave which can be approached carefully via a steep path. Continue on the track over a stretch of imitation Roman road. Go through a gate. Pass cottages on the left and an old walled garden on the right to arrive in front of the impressive **East Shaftoe Hall**.

3 At East Shaftoe Hall turn right to follow a long and very clear track which initially follows a fence on the left. Continue on through a gate and then over extensive pasture. Cross a footbridge and a ladder stile and keep on to join a tarmac road. Turn left along this, go through a gate and walk past **West Tofthill Cottage** on the left. Go through another gate and past **Sandyford Farm** over on the left. At a fork keep right but then bear left off the track to follow a public bridleway sign for **Belsay** over pasture. Aim towards the roof of **Shortflatt Tower**. Incidentally, if you followed the road round to the right, it would take you to **Harnham**, with its Buddhist monastery and historic **Harnham Hall**. Cross a stream over the footbridge and stile then go through a gate.

Harnham Hall stands on a very pronounced hill. In 1667 it came into the hands of Major Babbington, governor of Berwick. He was married to the beautiful Katherine, widow of Colonel George Fenwick of Brinkburn and daughter of Sir Arthur Haselrigg, Parliamentary ring-leader in the Civil War. She was so opposed to the Anglican church that in 1643 she paid the son of a blacksmith to pull the vicar out of his pulpit during a service. When the Restoration occurred the affronted vicar returned and excommunicated them. When Kate died she could not be buried in consecrated ground so in 1670 she was placed in a sepulchre hewn from the rock beneath Harnham. Her bones are no longer there but there is still a coffin in the cave in the 'tomb garden'. Shortflatt Tower, a very picturesque building was originally a pele tower, crenellated in 1305. It belonged to the wealthy Raymes family who also owned Aydon Castle near Corbridge.

4 After the gate, don't turn left along the public footpath but follow the bridleway sign alongside a wooden fence on the left. Then turn left through a gate into the paddock. Turn half right and ahead through another wicket gate into a wood. Keep on to exit via another gate. Turn right to go through a gate in a wall. Now turn left and follow this wall as it bends round to the left. Keep on through a wide gate, then on through another two. At the next facing fence at three oak trees turn right and follow the left field edge

THE PIPER'S CHAIR

down. Pass a hillock on the right. Go through a wide gate then cross a track and go through another. Follow the left field edge. Go through another wide gate and keep on along the left field edge. Cross a footbridge and go through a wicket gate. Now keep up the right side of the last field. At the end turn right through a wide gate then left through another to walk past the farmhouse, **Saugh House**, and barns. Exit to the A696 and turn left along this fast, narrow and dangerous road. You soon leave it at a complex junction where you cross over to walk down a very

quiet lane. At the end of this is a T-junction. Here you could turn right and walk into **Belsay**. The **Blacksmith's coffee shop** is at the entrance to **Belsay Hall and Castle** (English Heritage).

5 To continue the walk – at the T-junction cross over the road to go through a wide gate onto a bridleway (with hidden sign) to **Bolam church**. Follow the right field edge down a track. Faced by two wide gates take the left one and keep on down the left field edge. Keep on through another wide gate to cross a footbridge then head up along the left field edge. Go through a gate and along the next left field edge. Go through a wide double gate and keep on down a track. At a track junction, keep over and through a wide gate to follow the left field edge. At the crest of the field bear right a bit (note the ridge and furrow in this field) towards a house in the distance. Descend past gorse to cross a well-hidden footbridge, then turn left to go through an equally well-hidden wicket gate. Keep on up the left edge of the field along an avenue of trees and hawthorn bushes. Go through a wide gate and on along the left edge, through another gate and on along the left edge then down and through another two wide gates close together. Keep on through an ornate wrought-iron wicket gate and keep up a stony track along a left field edge.

6 Arriving at a double gate and private land sign turn right down the side of a copse then left through a wicket gate and right over a stone slab bridge. Now keep on up the field marked by lots of hillocks caused by quarrying. Pass a solitary

oak. Keep on alongside a stone wall and deep ditch to exit this stretch of parkland via a gate at a sign back to Belsay. Join a road here and turn left. If you wish you can turn right at a junction and visit **Bolam church**. Retrace your steps to the road and keep on, passing Bolam Hall and some cottages. At a T-junction, cross over and cross a stile into **Bolam Lake Country Park**. Keep on half left to the visitor centre.

Bolam's church has an impressive Saxon tower with classic Saxon features although much of the building is Norman, most notably the south doorway with its round arch and dog-tooth moulding, the chancel and the impressive chancel arch with its round pillars with scalloped capitals, and the south arcade. The rest is 13th-century. Don't miss the little window with plain glass which marks the point where on 1 May 1942 a German bomb entered the church but did not explode, and the fine half-length sandstone effigy of a knight with remaining traces of 14th-century colour. This may be Sir Walter de Bolam or Sir Richard de Raymes.

 Date walk completed:

SEATON SLUICE, ST MARY'S LIGHTHOUSE, HOLYWELL DENE AND SEATON SANDS

THE PICTURESQUE SEATON SLUICE HARBOUR

Distance:
10 miles

Map: OS Explorer 316 Newcastle upon Tyne

Starting Point:
The Waterford
Arms at Seaton
Sluice. GR 337767

How to get there: *Seaton Sluice is 9 miles north-east of Newcastle and a couple of miles north of Whitley Bay, on the A193. There is roadside parking at the harbour.*

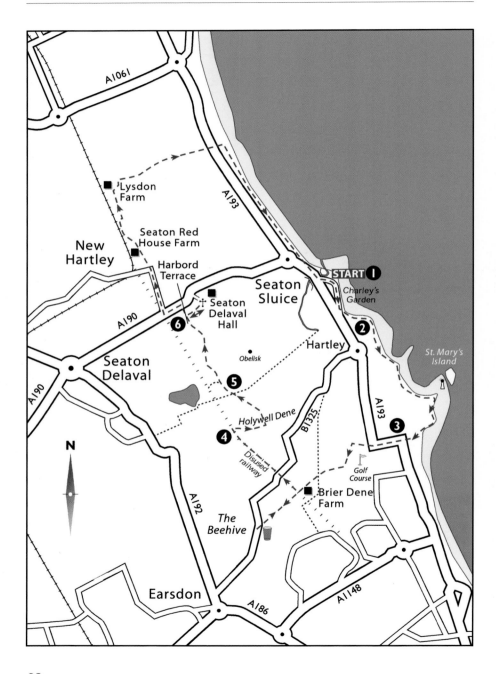

*S*tart from remarkable harbour works which were once central to a major industrial complex. Then enjoy a bracing cliff-top walk past the unusual Charley's Garden and on to the eyecatching St Mary's Lighthouse. The return section is quite different because much of it is across fields and along field edges. You cross the attractive Holywell Dene and encounter Seaton Delaval Hall, the home of the 'mad Delavals', a bijou Norman chapel and the site of one of the worst mining disasters in British history. Seaton Sands is the final stretch back to Seaton Sluice. A brief excursion from the circular route will take you to the old Beehive pub. This is a walk with everything!

The **Beehive Inn** is an imposing red brick building standing alone on the road from Earsdon. It has been an inn since 1890 but is on the site of a much older farm building which dated back some 300 years. The interior is labyrinthine, dark and beamed and has low door lintels so watch your head. There is a lovely beer garden and plenty of tables on the grass around the large car park. It offers a wide menu including the Infamous Beehive Grill. There is also a good range of snacks such as filled baps, basket meals and kids' baskets. There is a decent vegetarian range rather than the usual token item. As well as John Smith's there is always Morland's Old Speckled Hen and a guest ale.

The Beehive is open from 12 noon to 11 pm Monday to Saturday and 12 noon to 10.30 pm on Sunday. Food is available from 12 noon to 9 pm.

Telephone: *01912 529352*; www.beehiveInnearsdon.co.uk

The Walk

1 At the harbour walk towards the **King's Head**, passing an information board beside the remains of the rotating bridge mechanism. Walk to the left of the inn and onto the cliff-top path. Follow this as it winds round to the right behind houses between fences. At a road turn left and walk along the raised footway. Paths on the left lead down to the beach but keep on to a bench beside a footpath sign which says Coastline/Countryside. Turn left onto a good sandy path.

Seaton Sluice was once a great industrial complex with six great glass cones producing 145,000 dozen bottles a year and a railway to take them down to the harbour through a tunnel. The harbour dates from 1660 when Sir Ralph Delaval commissioned the construction of the harbour walls. Gates closed at high tide to hold back the Seaton Burn. At low tide the harbour floor was scoured by horse-drawn ploughs and the loose mud was washed away when the gates opened. On Sandy Island there were ballast hills derived from the ballast of returning collier brigs. The old harbour entrance was created in 1660 but was prone to silting – so sloops were only part loaded in the harbour and then taken out to deeper water to complete the loading using keel boats. The famous Cut was blasted out in 1761 by Tom Delaval to create a new harbour entrance. Rocky Island (where there were salt pans to produce salt from brine) was then entered by means of a rotating wooden bridge which allowed vessels to come through.

2 Follow this path along the coast, crossing a concrete track. Walk on past a caravan site. At a car park, keep left to rejoin the path and follow it alongside a cycleway. Where the path forks take the left fork and keep on. Then follow a low fence round to the right and rejoin the path which follows the line of the cycleway. Within yards follow it off to the left. At a fork, at an information board about the coastal grassland, turn left. Go down the path, cross a footbridge and continue on to benches overlooking **St Mary's Island**. Descend steps to join a concrete path parallel to the road, and turn right along this.

St Mary's Lighthouse was first lit in 1898. It replaced the Tynemouth Priory light. Access is via a causeway covered at high tide from Curry's Point where a Michael Curry was hanged in 1839 for murder. The lighthouse has 137 steps and was the last to be electrified, in 1977. Before that it was lit by means of a wick burning paraffin which was hoisted in cans to the top of the lighthouse by rope and pulley. In 1984 it was decommissioned and became the subject of a popular campaign which raised the money to buy it. In 1990 the Friends of St Mary's Lighthouse was formed to care for it.

3 At the main road cross over and walk ahead to a sharp right bend. Then continue on a track alongside a golf course and between the abutments of an old railway bridge. Turn left past this and follow the field edge to a stile on the right which you cross. Keep to the right field edge and cross a stile into a field. Cross this to the left end of the buildings of **Briar Dene Farm** then follow the track round them. Where the track bends right keep ahead over the field to the right corner to exit by a stile onto the former **Seaton Burn waggonway**. (If you should want to break here and visit the Beehive, cross the stile opposite and follow the right edge of two fields to cross a stile into the car park of the **Beehive**.) Turn right along the disused railway and follow this under a road bridge then past **Crow Hall Farm**. It enters **Holywell Dene** and crosses a high embankment through which the burn is culverted.

ST MARY'S LIGHTHOUSE

4 Approaching a stone bridge over the **Waggonways Cycle Route**, and just beyond a 'wagonways' sign made of old sleepers, turn right and cross a stile into **Holywell Dene**. Where the path forks at an information board, take the left fork. Now follow the woodland fringe to a stile. Cross this and turn right to follow the track. When you reach a wide gate on the left just past a hedge turn left through the gate and then follow the bridleway along the left field edge. At a track T-junction keep left and stay with the hedge on the left passing through two more fields.

Holywell Dene is old ravine woodland. Writer and historian, William Weaver Tomlinson wrote

of it '... a charming place for a picnic, as the visitors to the sea-side have long since discovered ... in the upper part, especially near the mill-dam, where the branches of lofty trees over-arch it, (are) some exquisite little pictures of sylvan loveliness.' There are red squirrels, badgers, kingfishers, great spotted woodpeckers and bullfinches. There used to be a healing spring dedicated to St Mary. The village and Dene were owned by the Delavals. The Dene was used for industries such a coal mining, charcoal burning and quarrying as well as for farming and milling. Since Victorian times it has been a resort for walkers.

5 At a complex crossways marked by a prominent post keep on ahead through a wide field gate and follow the raised grassy path. A tall obelisk is very prominent on the right. **Seaton Delaval Hall** is clear ahead to the right. Keep on through a wide gate. At **Holywell Farm**, keep on past another wide gate. Just past **Harbord Terrace** and just before the road called **The Avenue** turn right to visit the chapel crossing a stile on the left then keeping left round farm buildings on the right. Cross another stile onto a driveway and cross to go through a wall gap (or gate, if the hall is open).

This present hall was built in the early 18th century by Vanbrugh for the enterprising and eccentric Delavals who wanted to move away from their original hall which was too close to the industrial complex which they had developed and whence they derived the income to afford this hall. It suffered a bad fire in the early 19th century and has been only partly restored. It has lovely gardens. Also in the grounds is the little Norman chapel which dates to the 12th century. When the Delaval line became extinct, the estates descended to the Barons Hastings, with whom they remain.

6 Retrace your steps and turn right down to the main road. Turn left and walk to a right turn to **New Hartley**. At a sharp left turn, keep on along the bridleway lane to **Seaton Red**

House Farm, then along the gravel track to **Lysdon Farm** crossing a stile by a wide gate. At **Lysdon Farm** turn off right down a muddy enclosed track. This takes you through a wicket gate and into fields where you press on to a very wide gate and exit onto the A193. Cross over and either turn right onto a coastal track, or follow the path along the dunes, or cross over them onto the attractive beach. All ways will take you to **Seaton Sluice**. Having crossed the road bridge over the small harbour keep left and up to the very obvious **King's Head**.

Close to the route near New Hartley was the shaft of Hartley New Pit where, in January 1862, 204 miners died when the beam of the pumping engine snapped and fell down the single shaft at the moment when shifts were changing. There was no other exit so most of the men died of suffocation. The bodies were buried in Earsdon churchyard where there is a large memorial listing all the victims, including numerous members of individual families, very young boys and men in their 70s.

Date walk completed:

BROCOLITIA, THE BANKS OF THE SOUTH TYNE, WARDEN HILL AND CARR EDGE

THE SITE OF THE MITHRAEUM AT BROCOLITIA

Distance:
12 miles

Map: OS Explorer OL 43 Hadrian's Wall

Starting Point:
Brocolitia National
Park car park
(pay). GR 860713

How to get there: Brocolitia is 7 miles north-west of
Hexham on the B6318. From the A69 turn north along the
A6079 to join the B6318 near Chollerford then follow it
westwards.

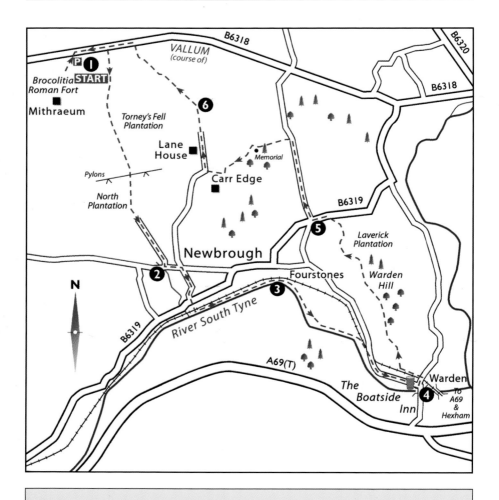

*T*his walk links the Roman Wall area to the Tyne valley. There are superb views along the valley from the flanks of Warden Hill. The silence of the long moorland stretch south of Brocolitia is disturbed only by the song of skylarks. You'll enjoy the walk along the banks of the South Tyne which is at its best here. On the way you encounter evidence of two remarkable cults which have affected the world in very different ways. Enjoy a break at the Boatside Inn at Warden as well.

The **Boatside Inn** at Bridge End was built in the early 19th century. Meals are served in the bar and lounge and also in the restaurant and conservatory. The main beers are Black Sheep, High House Auld Hemp, Mordue's and John Smith's, with various guest ales such as those of the Wylam and Consett breweries. There is a beer garden. The menu includes substantial and unpretentious food like home-made chicken pie, a good repertoire of steaks and fish dishes, a tempting succulent lamb shank, oven-roasted duck breast and Californian loin of pork. Vegetarians are well catered for with items like thyme, lime and asparagus risotto and five cheese cannelloni. There are also sandwiches. The prices are reasonable and the staff are very considerate.

The Boatside is open all day from 11 am on weekdays and 12 noon on Sundays. Food is served between 12 noon and 2 pm and from 6.30 pm to 9 pm on weekdays and 7 pm to 9 pm on Sundays.

Telephone: *01434 602233*; www.theboatsideinn.com

Note also the Red Lion in Newbrough (*telephone: 01434 674226*) and the Railway Inn in Fourstones (*telephone: 01434 674711*).

 The Walk

❶ After visiting the Mithraeum next to the Roman fort, return to the car park and turn right along the fast B6318 to a footpath sign and stone stile on the right. Cross over and follow the left field edge to two gates. Go through the left one. Follow the right field edge through a wide gate and up a rise. Ahead is a line of pylons. To the left is one close to a coniferous plantation. Aim for the pylon to the right of that, following an intermittent track and keeping half left. As you get closer aim for the left end of a conifer fringe beyond your marker pylon. Go through a wide gate and follow the left field edge through a gate at the left end of the plantation. Follow a track to a wooden cottage, and then a metalled lane. At the lane end turn left into **Newbrough**.

Brocolitia Fortress at Carrawburgh was built in AD 134 and was garrisoned until 383. It held 500 men. Mithras was an eastern sun god, born from heaven. On the 25 December he captured and killed a bull in a cave. This was the first animal created on earth. From its blood new life was created. The temple was intended to recreate the cave. At one end was a large painting or relief of Mithras killing the bull. There were three altars in front of it. The Mithraeum may have been destroyed by Christians faced with a dangerous rival. You can visit a virtual mithraeum on www.museums.ncl.ac.uk and a reconstruction of one in the Newcastle Museum of Antiquities.

2 Opposite the **Red Lion** turn right down a road which narrows into an enclosed lane. At a T-junction turn right then left down a drive signed Fourstones/Warden Bridge. Keep to the right of **Allerwash Mill** to go beneath a railway bridge where Meggie's Burn joins the Tyne. The path winds round to the left and over rocks then becomes a gravelled path along the banks of the **South Tyne**. The railway line is on the left and the river down below on the right. Keep right at a fork and stay on the riverside path through a silver birch wood. Exit onto an open grassy area in front of a cottage and outhouses. Follow the path in front of these and keep on to arrive at **Riverside Cottage**.

The banks of the South Tyne are most attractive and inviting on calm sunny days. However, it has the record for the highest flood flow on any river in England and Wales when, in 1771, the Great Flood destroyed thirteen out of fourteen bridges on the Tyne and South Tyne. Only the bridge at

Corbridge survived. There have been disastrous floods on the Tyne throughout history. It has a very high water velocity because it travels a shorter distance than most rivers between source and mouth, and has a steeper slope.

3 Pass in front of the cottage between a fence on the left and trees on the right. The path narrows and is often overgrown. At a freestanding stile (bank erosion has produced a diversion here) keep on with the fence on the left then with a wall on the right. Cross a ladder stile on the right. Cross a pleasant meadow passing a small enclosed area with a stile and wide gate. At a facing fence cross a stile and keep on. Beware of rabbit holes. The path follows a sort of low concrete wall on the left then crosses it. Finally walk up through a patch of woodland away from the river to the road. Turn right along the road to Warden passing **Fourstones Paper Mill** (1763) and cottages to arrive at the **Boatside Inn** at **Bridge End**.

There was an important fording point here as long ago as 1298, and an ancient manorial ferry boat – hence the inn on the boatside. At a later date a chain bridge was used by cattle drovers. In 1826 a suspension bridge was constructed and the old toll house still survives. The present bridge was built in 1903. The name Warden is

THE BOATSIDE INN AT THE HALFWAY POINT OF THE WALK

derived from the Old English **weard dun** *meaning* watch hill. *The hill has been the site of an Iron Age hill fort, a medieval village and possibly a Roman camp. Certainly the view from Warden Hill is spectacular. The church is notable for its Anglo-Saxon tower. It is near Warden where the North and South Tynes meet.*

4 From the **Boatside Inn** turn left under the railway bridge then left along a signed footpath near a lay-by. Stay on this to **Quality Cottages**. At a signpost turn right for **Fourstones** up to a wicket gate.

Through this follow the left field edge. Go through another wicket gate. Turn left through a wide gate and follow a track briefly. Continue along a right field edge with good views along the Tyne valley, including the Fourstones Paper Mill. Go through a wide gate and keep on towards a wood on the flank of **Warden Hill**. Go through a wide gate then follow the left field edge to go through another wide gate. Follow the bridleway sign to Fourstones. Stay with the path at the edge of the wood passing a bridleway sign to Warden which would take you to the top of **Warden Hill**. Keep on, following a sign to Whinney Hill/Fourstones. Go through a wide gate to exit the wood. Follow a wall on the left to a cottage and join a gravel track. Go left through a wide gate. At a signpost stay with the Whinney Hill sign and on the track. Beyond a power station exit onto a road and turn left.

5 Keep on to a T-junction. Turn right for **Wark/Bellingham**. Now follow a quiet road for nearly a mile to a wide gate on the left by a bridleway sign to Carr Edge Only. Follow the track into woodland via a gate. At a fork divert left to see the scout memorial (be careful at the edge of the rock outcrop). Return to the fork and follow the path to a wide gate. Go through and bear left towards **Carr Edge Farm**. It can be quite boggy near a small stream. Keep on the near side until you join a grassy track crossing the stream. Go up to the farm and through a wide gate. Keep on through two more wide gates past barns and turn right between the barns and the back of the farmhouse. Follow the farm drive as it winds round to a junction via a wide gate. Turn right and follow the gravel lane past **Lane House** and through a couple of wide gates past **Torney's Fell**. Keep on past various discarded farm vehicles and, through a wide gate, up a grassy track with a wall on the left. This can be badly overgrown. At the end cross a ladder stile next to a wide gate.

All the histories of Scouting refer to Humshaugh in Northumberland as the site of the first official camp in 1908, the year when Scouting for Boys *was published. The real site was here, at Carr Edge. A dalek-shaped cairn commemorates this great event: 'This cairn marks the site of the first boy scout camp held in 1908 by BP, later Lord Baden-Powell of Gilwell, Chief Scout of the World'. Other plaques have been added to mark later events and anniversaries. It is a very atmospheric place.*

6 Bear half left across the moorland. On the right you will see a fine limekiln. Keep on past a solitary large boulder and a patch of gorse on the left. Across a rise descend to a facing fence and cross a stile next to a wide gate. Keep on towards the right end of a plantation. Cross a stile next to a wide gate. Now head north past a walled enclosure and house over on the left. Cross the **Vallum** and then exit via a stile by a wide gate on to the fast B6318. Now turn left along this and return to **Brocolitia**.

Date walk completed:

DONKLEYWOOD, GREENHAUGH, BLACK MIDDENS AND KIELDER FOREST

THE RUINS OF BLACK MIDDENS BASTLE

Distance: 11 miles	**Map: OS Explorer OL 42 Kielder Water & Forest**
Starting Point: *Donkleywood. GR 746864*	**How to get there:** *Donkleywood is 2 miles east of Falstone. Follow the Border County Ride off the B6320 leading into Bellingham from the south. There is some roadside parking at Donkleywood.*

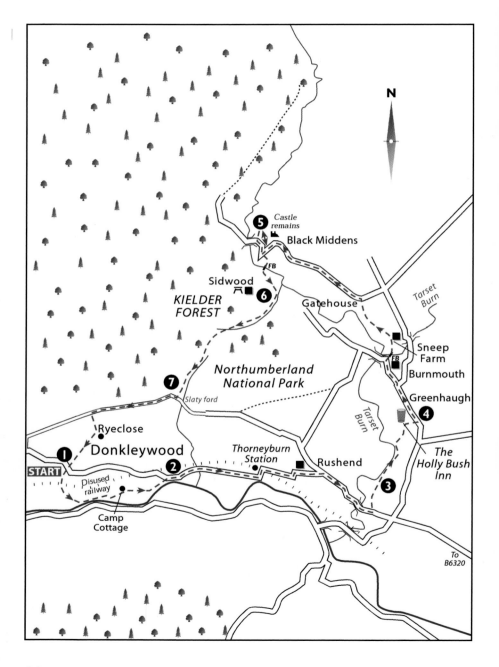

*T*his area was the scene of recurrent border reiving for 300 years. That explains the density of defensive farmhouses or 'bastles'. On this walk you see several of them. For part of it you follow the Reivers' Way. However, the most striking feature of the route is the largest man-made woodland in Europe, Kielder Forest, or at least an edge of it. At various points you meet the pretty Tarset Burn and the North Tyne, the latter making its way from Kielder Water, the largest lake in Britain. There are no great gradients but there are some excellent views. There are stretches along quiet and scenic country lanes.

Dating from 1650, the **Holly Bush Inn** is the oldest building in Greenhaugh. Its great claim to fame is that it was the only North Tyne public house not to run out of beer during the Second World War. There is a good menu which changes frequently. Choose from the board then enjoy. The regular real ale is Nel's Best from the High House Farm Brewery. There is usually at least one other real ale on offer.

The Holly Bush is open from 5 pm to 11 pm Monday to Friday and 12 noon to 11 pm on Saturday and Sunday. Food is usually available until 9 pm.

Telephone: *01434 240391*; www.hollybushinn.net

 The Walk

1 In **Donkleywood** at the village green cross a ladder stile at a sign for **Camp Cottage**. Follow the track past cottages and through a wide gate. At two wide gates go through the right one and cross a bridge over a dismantled railway. Bear half left diagonally over the field past an isolated oak to a stile by a wide gate. Cross the stile and follow a woodland path alongside the **North Tyne**. Exit over a stile. Then keep on to cross another high stile. Follow the fence on your right to cross another stile and follow another right field edge. Just before **Camp Cottage** turn right across a stile then wind round in front of it to cross another stile into a field. Bear half right then cross a stile into an immature plantation. Follow the left edge to cross another high stile. Now follow a half left line to cross a step stile and descend into a little valley. Cross a footbridge and go up to cross a stile onto a road at a sign back to Donkleywood.

Donkleywood is one of the oldest documented settlements in North Tynedale. In 1166 Duncliushalch was recorded as the site of a hunting lodge of William the Lion of Scotland who held the Liberty of Tynedale from the English kings. By 1279 it was one of the seven main townships in the area – when it was recorded as being fined 20 shillings in conjunction with Thorneyburne and Tarsethope for decapitating a thief without waiting for a coroner's trial! On your route from here is a section of the former Border Counties Railway which arrived in 1860 long before a good road was built so it was the lifeline of the valley.

2 Turn right along this quiet gated road. It rises and bends to the left at a stile and footpath signed The Hott. Continue on past **Thorneyburn Station** then **Rushend**. At a fork where a road joins from the left keep on ahead down to the old road bridge. Cross over and walk up the bank. Past **Redmire Cottages** turn left at a sign for Greenhaugh. Go through three wide gates then bear half left through a gap in a ruined fence and across the next field to a wicket gate. Go through and half left to descend to a kissing gate and the **Tarset Burn**.

3 Go through and follow the path close to the burn through another wicket gate, over a footbridge, then along a board section. Keep on through another kissing gate beside a wide gate. Go through the next field and through the next kissing gate. Now keep on along the bottom of a sloping field and through a wicket gate. Cross another sloping field skirting round a boggy section. Enter woodland. Go through another kissing gate and follow a fence on the right. Keep on past the end of a footbridge on the left then cross a footbridge over a side stream. Turn right up a wide track then a metalled lane. Exit to a road via a wide gate near a Greenhaugh Village sign. Turn left for the **Holly Bush Inn** and **Greenhaugh**.

Greenhaugh's name derives from the common Northumbrian word 'haugh' which means a stretch of flat land by a river or in a valley bottom. In medieval times the village served the drove road which ran through it linking farms in England with markets across the border. Until the Second World War most of the villagers were employed on the Greenhaugh Hall and Sidwood estates.

4 From the **Holly Bush** turn left along the quiet road. Pass a junction on the right. Keep on to **Burnmouth** and the **Low Tarset Linn**. Cross a ladder stile next to a wide gate

signed Sneep Farm/
Gatehouse. Descend to
the left to cross a
footbridge. Follow the
fence on the right initially
then go up a bank past a
waymarked post and
through a wide gate. Bear
half left across a field
through another wide
gate and along a track
past **Sneep Farm**. Go
through another wide
gate and between barns.

THE HOLLY BUSH INN DATES FROM THE 17TH CENTURY

If access to the stile is
blocked by barbed wire,
go through a wide gate. Keep on
over the field to descend the bank to
cross a stile and footbridge and up
into the next field. Follow the left
edge. Cross a step stile and keep on
between fences to go through a wide
gate. Follow the track as it bears
round right to **Gatehouse**. Cross a
ladder stile and go out onto a road.
Turn left then walk on for a mile to
Black Middens.

*Bastles were fortified farmhouses
with living quarters on the top
floor reached only by means of a
ladder which could be pulled up.
The farm animals would be driven
onto the ground floor. There were
over 70 bastles along the border,
all built within hailing distance of
each other. Black Middens is in the
care of English Heritage. In the
little hamlet of Gatehouse there
are two bastles, including North*

*Gatehouse which is probably the
best in the county. It has scarcely
been changed since it was built in
the late 16th century.*

❺ From **Black Middens** retrace
your steps. At a sharp bend to the
left go through a wide gate with a
public footpath sign. Walk along the
rough track to the field end. Turn
right along the fence to cross a
footbridge and follow a sign to
Sidwood car park turning left
through a kissing gate to follow a
path alongside the **Tarset Burn**. This
is the **Reiver's Way**. Go through
another kissing gate and on through
old mixed woodland. The path winds
to the right and rises to join a track
at **Sidwood**. Turn left for a few
yards. Don't turn off right at a Green
Trail indicated by a marker post.
Keep on and opposite the picnic site
turn right at a bridleway sign for

Slaty Ford. Follow this clear path as it rises and bears left to arrive at a forestry track.

Kielder Forest covers 250 square miles between the Scottish Border and the South Tyne. Planting started in 1926 to build up a strategic national reserve of timber. The bulk of the land was originally owned by the Church Commissioners but was bought by the Forestry Commission. In recent years there has been a greater emphasis on its value as a recreational and ecological asset. Sidwood House was originally built in 1743 and was at the centre of a 5000-acre estate. However, when the last family to own it became bankrupt the Forestry Commission bought it. The white Sidwood Lodge is the only part of the house which remains, the rest was demolished.

6 Don't cross over to follow the obvious path ahead. Instead turn right and walk past a track to the left and the end of a small stream valley. Then turn left up an unsigned and rather faint path. This becomes more pronounced as it heads up alongside the developing valley and between heather and bracken. At another forestry track cross over and follow the clear sandy path between plantations. It levels out and arrives at a fence corner and a ruined wall. With the fence and wall

on your left keep ahead through a bridleway marked wide gate. Follow the faint path half right. It moves away from the fence/wall and follows the side of a valley on your left. Keep on through a young plantation then cross a burn and boggy area as best you can to continue up to a sign back to Sidwood and join a clear track.

7 Turn right and follow the track round to the left alongside a fence. Cross a burn and keep on through a couple of wide gates to arrive at **Ryeclose** and a high gate on the left. Go through the gate and down the track. At **Ryeclose** go through a wide gate on its right then bear half left through another wide gate and cross a hidden ladder stile. Keep on across a step stile and continue half left across a little valley passing a marker post. Be careful in the broken ground here. Keep on up to cross a stile by a wide gate and keep half left downhill to cross a high step stile. Follow a short fence on the right to cross a step stile by a wide gate, go through another wide gate then cross a stile and go through a wall gap to reach the road at **Donkleywood**.

Date walk completed:

BARDON MILL, VINDOLANDA, ONCE BREWED AND HOUSESTEADS

CRAG LOUGH SEEN FROM HIGHSHIELD CRAGS

Distance:
10½ miles

Map: OS Explorer OL 43 Hadrian's Wall

Starting Point:
*Bardon Mill
village centre.
GR 779647*

How to get there: *Bardon Mill stands just off the A69 between Haydon Bridge and Haltwhistle. You can park in the village centre.*

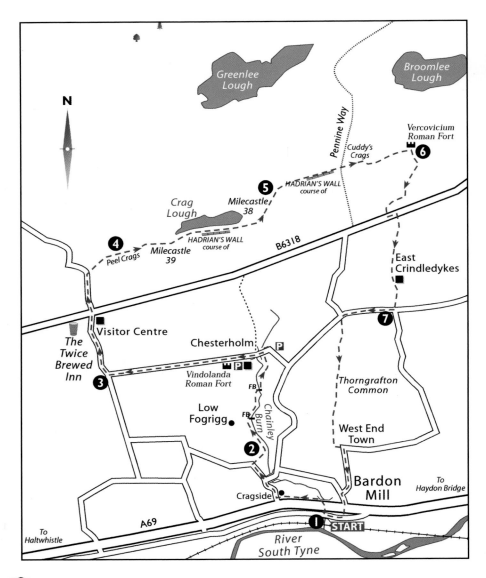

The present **Twice Brewed** dates from the 19th century but there were inns near here as early as 1696. It may be so-called because this stretch of drovers' road was between two hills or *brews*. In 1934 Lane End Farm was given to the YHA and it was converted into a Youth Hostel called Once

Brewed to indicate less potent beverages! Confusingly the settlement is officially called Once Brewed. Ales include Twice Brewed Bitter, Boddingtons and various guest cask ales from the High House Farm and Allendale breweries. The same menu, with a good range, is available in both bar and restaurant. The bar menu also offers baguettes and main courses including Northumbrian beef and Guinness cobbler, home-made steak pie and Northumbrian farmhouse sausages. There is a beer garden.

The Twice Brewed is open from 11 am to 11 pm on Monday to Saturday and 12 noon to 10.30 pm on Sunday.

Telephone: *01434 344534*; www.twicebrewedinn.co.uk

---

*M*uch of the outward journey is along the quiet Chainley Dene and then, beyond the famous Roman remains and museum of Vindolanda, a steady march along quiet lanes to the attractions of the Twice Brewed Inn. Thence follow a famous section of the Roman Wall on the Whin Sill to arrive at an impressive Roman fortress having enjoyed spectacular views along the Wall and across its loughs. The final section heads south traversing a series of lesser volcanic basalt ripples back to the South Tyne and Bardon Mill with its prominent pottery.

 *The Walk*

1 From the village enter the grounds of **Bardon Mill Pottery** and ascend a slope. The right of way is a tarmac path sloping to the left. Go up to arrive at the busy A69. Cross carefully to a signpost to Henshaw. Follow a tree-lined track to a wicket gate. Go through and follow the right field edge. Through a kissing gate turn left along a track through a wide gate to a quiet road. Turn right and, at a junction, turn left and up the bank to **Cragside Stables**. The right of way goes over a stone stile and across a field to a gate but the stile is now separated from the field by a fence. Just follow the drive past barns. Bear round and down the track to enter the dene of the **Chainley Burn**.

2 Keep on to **Low Fogrigg**, then cross a footbridge and bear right on a path above the burn. Go through a field gate and cross a field. Go through a gate then along a grassy path which descends and follows the stream more closely. Go through a wooden gap stile then on along boardwalk sections and through two more stiles. You arrive at a gate into **Vindolanda**. Cross a footbridge beside this then follow the path round the right side of the fence enjoying a good view of **Chesterholm**. The path rises and reaches a driveway. Continue on to a very quiet road. Turn left along this and keep on, crossing a footbridge/ford and enjoying glimpses of **Vindolanda** on the left. Follow this straight road, past one of a few Roman milestones still in situ.

Vindolanda fort covered 3½ acres. A pre-Wall Stanegate fortress, it probably dates to around AD 85 but underwent several rebuildings before being abandoned in the 4th century. West of the fort was the civilian settlement or vicus which included a bath house and married quarters. At Vindolanda today there are reconstructions of wooden and stone turrets. Recently-discovered, partly burnt letters and records tell a lot about everyday life and garrison routines on the Wall.

3 At a junction turn right for **Once Brewed**. At the **National Park Visitor Centre** turn left over the car park and along a path to the **Twice Brewed**. Thence resume your walk by turning right back along the fast road. At a sign to Steel Rigg turn left. Just past the **Peel Bothy** cross a ladder stile (signed Hadrian's Wall and Housesteads). Cross a field bearing left to another ladder stile. Cross this and then go through a wicket gate, passing a National Trust sign. Cross a stile and follow a paved path and steps up the end of **Peel Crags**. At the top of the crag cross a ladder stile and start off along a good gravel path along the Wall. You can see Crag Lough in the distance.

It was while he was staying at an older inn at East Twice Brewed that septuagenarian William Hutton, walking the Wall both ways in 1801, sat amazed at dinner as he watched the carriers eat. Hutton was a remarkable man who had been a factory boy and became a book dealer and author. He remarked in his diary (later published as The History of the Roman Wall) *that he saw them consume boiled beef equal to about half a beast, followed by a pudding equal to a peck measure and washed down with ale in gulps each of which would be enough to last a man for a whole meal. Incidentally the mortar used along the Wall by the Romans has lasted for 18 centuries and it is believed that the secret ingredient was 60 per cent animal fat, which is a lot of carcasses and an amazing stench!*

4 Follow the Roman Wall path across two steep dips. In the bottom of the second, **Castle Nick**, is **Milecastle 39**. Continue as the path bends right and descends into a third and bigger dip. At the bottom is a well and the famous Robin's Sycamore shown in Kevin Costner's *Robin Hood, Prince of Thieves*. Past the tree turn left through a gap in the Wall then continue up steps onto **Highshield Crags**, passing a good example of basalt columns. Cross a ladder stile and follow a gravel path high above **Crag Lough**. There is no fence on the left and there are sheer drops. Continue through a wood to exit via a ladder stile. Keep on to cross another ladder stile near a National Trust sign. Cross a wide track and cross another ladder stile. Now follow the path round to **Milecastle 38** and **Hotbank Farm**.

There are four glacial loughs in the Wall area – Grinton, Crag, Broomlee and Greenlee. They were formed by the scouring effect of ice sheets during the last Ice Age, the same force which turned the basalt 'ripple' into crags. They are all gradually shrinking because of the deposition of organic matter by the loughside vegetation which slowly accumulates and rises above the water level. This process is called succession. It is especially obvious at Crag Lough.

THE CONFUSINGLY-NAMED TWICE BREWED AT ONCE BREWED!

5 Keep on across another ladder stile and up the bank. Pass a small wood on the left and continue to a point where you can see the other Wall loughs. To the north is **Greenlee Lough**, to the north-east is **Broomlee Lough** and to the south-east is **Grinton Lough**. Descend into **Rapishaw Gap** and cross a ladder stile. Pass the **Pennine Way** ladder stile on the left and cross a ladder stile ahead. Keep on over the next dip and up to **Cuddy's Crags**. Pass **Milecastle 37**, with its well-preserved section of arch, then enter a small copse via a wicket gate. Turn left and ascend some stone steps, then walk along this very scenic section of Wall to exit near **Housesteads Fort** via a wicket gate on the right.

Housesteads is one of the seventeen forts of Hadrian's Wall. It was built in the period

AD 122–130, overwhelmed on several occasions and restored, but abandoned after AD 383 when a final disaster seems to have overcome it. The fort exhibits the usual rectangular plan and layout of Roman camps and forts, with four great gateways on each side in a wall around a compound of five acres sub-divided by a network of streets. Blocks of buildings include a headquarters building, the Commandant's house, two granaries, a hospital and barrack blocks sub-divided into pairs of rooms for sections of eight to ten men. The drainage and water supply system includes an impressive latrine block.

6 Walk down the side of the fortress and pass in front of the ticket office to join a track which slants diagonally to the right in front of **Housesteads Farm**. Cross another basalt 'ripple' to exit onto the B6318 road via a wide gate. Cross carefully and turn left for a few yards before going over a ladder stile (bridleway sign). Follow a grassy path ahead over a series of ripples. At the top of the first crest, where the path seems to disappear, bear right to pick up a clear track again up the next ridge. Keep on ahead up to a bridleway marker post. Descend to pass through a couple of gates with **East Crindledykes Farm** on the left. Follow the farm road up to a quiet minor road (the old Stanegate, in fact).

7 Turn right and follow the road past one junction and on to a second. Follow the Bardon Mill sign round to the left. At a signpost for Thorngrafton go through a kissing gate and follow a grassy track up over a saddle. At the top over on the right is the site of a Roman signal station which you can visit along a clear path. You get a good view across **Vindolanda**. Returning to the original point look for a stone gap stile. Go through and head downhill over **Thorngrafton Common**. Bear slightly right to reach a marker post with two right-of-way options. Take the one on the right and follow an increasingly pronounced track with a linear plantation over on the right. Arriving at an enclosure corner ignore the confusing markers and walk down an enclosed track. Cross a ladder stile and keep on to **West End Town** then turn left along the lane towards Thorngrafton. At a junction turn right and follow a quiet road down to **Bardon Mill**. At the war memorial turn right to return to the village centre (with the **Bowes Hotel** just beyond).

Date walk completed:

HALTWHISTLE, FEATHERSTONE CASTLE, THE LAMBLEY VIADUCT AND THE SOUTH TYNE TRAIL

THE IMPRESSIVE LAMBLEY VIADUCT

Distance: 10½ miles	Map: OS Explorer OL 43 Hadrian's Wall
Starting Point: *The Black Bull in Haltwhistle. GR 707642*	**How to get there:** *Haltwhistle is just off the A69 halfway between Brampton and Haydon Bridge. Park in the free car park in Lanty's Lonnen. There is also some roadside parking.*

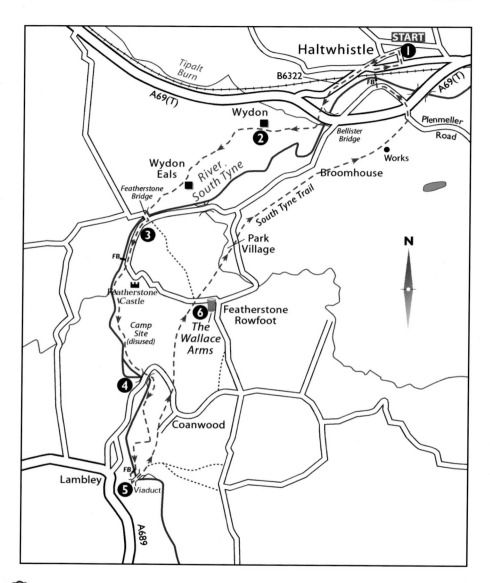

The **Wallace Arms** in Featherstone is a stone-built whitewashed country inn with a beer garden. Inside is a small public bar, a restaurant area and a games room. It is stone-floored and not modernised out of character. The main real ales are Greene King's Abbot Ale and IPA, as well as frequently changed guest ales. It has an extensive menu with a good range of seafood dishes, grills and chicken dishes and an excellent steak and real ale pie. There is a good vegetarian menu and children's menu. The welcoming Wallace supplies Sunday lunches virtually any time from 12 noon to 9 pm! It also does all-day breakfasts and has a full range of snacks and specials. There is a takeaway menu.

The Wallace Arms is open all day in summer. Lunch is served 12 noon to 2 pm, afternoon tea 3 pm to 5 pm, and evening meals 5 pm to 9 pm. Winter opening times are 12 noon to 3 pm and 6 pm to 9 pm Tuesday to Thursday, and 12 noon to 11 pm Friday to Monday.

Telephone: *01434 321872*; www.thewallacearms.co.uk

---

*T*he theme of this walk must be railways and bridges. There is a long stretch along the South Tyne Trail which follows the disused railway, with the whitewashed Wallace Arms halfway, and a range of interesting road and rail bridges, including the famous Lambley Viaduct and the scenic Featherstone Bridge. Much of the route passes through pleasant fields and woodland in the valley of the South Tyne and there you will encounter the impressive Featherstone Castle and the remains of a Second World War prison camp.

 *The Walk*

❶ From the **Black Bull** turn left down **Main Street** past the **Haltwhistle War Memorial Hospital**. Follow the road round to the left. Cross over near the railway station then turn right along **West Road**. Keep on across the railway bridge then along **Tyne View Road**. At a road junction, opposite a bus shelter and small field, turn left then immediately fork off to the right down a short lane. At the end of this, with **Bellister Bridge** (pedestrianised) on the left, keep ahead down an enclosed lane. At the end turn left at a footpath sign to walk alongside the A69 bypass road. Descend steps to go beneath the road then continue along the path to exit via a stile onto a lane (a continuation of the original one). Turn left and follow the lane to **Wydon Farm** crossing the **Tipalt Burn**.

THE WALLACE ARMS MAKES A WELCOME STOP
ON THE ROUTE

the wide track through a couple of gates to exit onto a road where you turn left to cross the scenic **Featherstone Bridge**.

The South Tyne floods quickly and easily. The fine bridge with its single lofty arch, which is so popular with artists, fishermen and picnickers, is the version built in 1778. An earlier attempt was washed away in 1771. The Great Flood of 1771 destroyed every bridge on the Tyne except for that at Corbridge. At various points you can see how the riverbank has had to be built up to counteract erosion. Upstream from the bridge is a Northumbrian Water Company gauging station which records the speed with which the South Tyne rises and falls and enables an early warning to be given about the danger of flooding. There is also a salmon leap. Adult salmon can leap about 11 feet.

2 Go through a series of wide gates through the farm to reach an old cart track. Follow the track, going through another wide gate, as it rises and bends left. At a couple of gates at right angles to each other keep on ahead through the facing one and along the right field edge. Through another gate keep on ahead across the field towards the far right corner passing the ends of a couple of small gullies. In the field corner cross a stile then follow the left field edge. Just past a depression at the bottom end of the field turn left over a stile into a woodland fringe. Follow the winding path through open woodland to a wide gate. Go through then follow the left enclosure edge to reach a stony track. Turn left towards **Wydon Eals**. Cross a stile by a gate and keep through another gate. Now follow

3 Across the bridge turn right then follow the quiet road alongside the Tyne. Just past the Featherstone footbridge go through a wicket gate on the right (signed public bridleway 300 yards then public footpath/Diamond Oak). Follow the lovely grassy path by the river. **Featherstone Castle** is on the left. At a waymarked post join a tarmac track and keep on through gateposts. Follow the track which was the main road through a wartime prison camp.

Pass old concrete posts, the concrete bases of huts and brick buildings. Keep on through a wide gate, and near a modern road bridge exit onto the road via a wicket gate.

Featherstone Castle is first mentioned in the reign of Henry III in the 13th century. It was held by the Featherstone family for twelve generations. The castle is one of the most attractive strongholds in the north and is said to be haunted by a ghostly bridal party. Featherstone Park POW Camp 18 held German officers from 1945 to 1948. Up to 7,000 prisoners were housed in 100 huts guarded by 200 soldiers. After the war many of the Germans worked on local farms and were well liked. They even had their own newspaper printed at Hexham, Die Ziet am Tyne.

4 Cross the road and follow a sign to **Coanwood** through a wicket gate. Follow a pleasant path with the river over on your right. Cross a small stream on a plank bridge and keep on. When the path peters out, continue on the same line. Aim for an isolated house half left, crossing another plank bridge in a boggy area. Cross a rocky drive and go behind the house to cross a small bridge. Cross the field diagonally to the far left corner by the river and go through a wicket gate to follow the narrow woodland path with the river

to the right. Soon the **Lambley Viaduct** looms above you. Cross an impressive footbridge on the right over the **South Tyne** and climb the steps to the viaduct which you cross.

The Lambley Viaduct was the final link in the Haltwhistle–Alston branch railway. It was built by the Newcastle and Carlisle Railway Company at a point where the fells rise up from the river to the 2,000 ft plateau of Cold Fell. Designed by Sir George Barclay-Bruce, it was opened in November 1852. It has been described as 'the most impressive monument of railway enterprise and optimism in the branch lines of Northumberland'. It is built of sandstone from Slaggyford and Bardon Mill and carried lead, coal and limestone from Alston Moor. There are nine main arches each with a 17-metre span, and seven smaller arches each with a 6-metre span carrying the trackbed 32 metres above the South Tyne. It was restored in 1995–96.

5 Go through the gate at the end of the viaduct and walk along the track. Go through a wicket gate and cross another track to continue along the railway track through a gate. Pass a station platform and a big white house. **Coanwood** is over on the right. At a wicket gate cross a road and keep on. Follow the track through a cutting under a bridge then through a kissing gate. Pass a pond over on the left. Go through another kissing gate then via another gate onto the road near **Featherstone Park Station car park**. Turn right up the road for the **Wallace Arms**.

6 To continue, cross the road to **Station House** and stay on the trail, following a sign for Park Village. Pass the station platform. Keep on through a wide gate and a deep cutting. Go through another wide gate then across a steep embankment lined with silver birches. At a fork keep right, rather than up to **Park Village**. Keep on beneath a bridge, up to a wicket gate and across a road to continue along the track which, after open fields on both sides, enters a long stretch of shallow cuttings. Keep on under another bridge and between abutments then past **Broomhouse** on the left. Keep on under a bridge and on past a small pond on the right into more open country. Pass an extensive factory area on the right. Now you can see north over the Tyne and up to Wall country. Keep on under another bridge and through a stretch of woodland and along an embankment to reach **Plenmeller Road**. Cross the road then turn left to descend to the busy A69. Cross this very carefully then continue down the road opposite (a No Through Road). At a junction before a house turn right and walk to cross

the **Tyne** on an iron humpback bridge. Go under a small railway viaduct and on up **Lanty's Lonnen** into **Haltwhistle**.

It may be all memorial gardens and well-tended flower beds today but Haltwhistle was once at the centre of the ongoing raiding, arson and murdering by the border reivers. This explains the prevalence of castles and fortified bastle houses in the area. There are six castles encircling Haltwhistle – Bellister, Blenkinsopp, Thirlwall, Featherstone, Langley and Bewcastle. It has five bastle houses – more than any other town – and one fortified pele tower, now the Centre of Britain Hotel. Haltwhistle stands in picturesque scenery but has a very active industrial history. There were limekilns, brickworks, a drift mine and a woollen mill. The name, incidentally, is derived from the Old French Haut Wisel which means high ground between two rivers, and is inspired by the fact that the settlement stands in a fork of the South Tyne and the Haltwhistle Burn.

Date walk completed:

BYWELL, CHERRYBURN, PRUDHOE CASTLE AND OVINGHAM

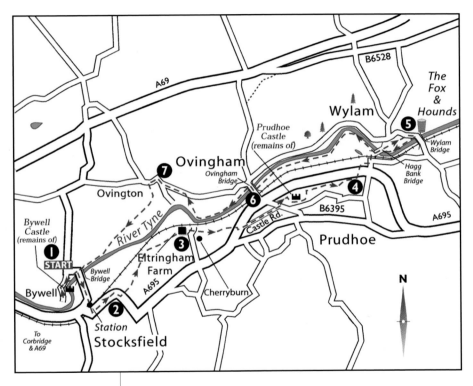

Distance:
12 miles

Map: OS Explorer 316 Newcastle upon Tyne

Starting Point:
Bywell.
GR 049615

How to get there: *Bywell is 4 miles south-east of Corbridge. From the A69 take the B6309 south towards Stocksfield. Park by the roadside near either St Peter's or St Andrew's church.*

PRUDHOE CASTLE SEEN AMONGST THE TREES

*T*his is a journey through time, as well as the Tyne valley. In Bywell alone you encounter two historic churches, a castle and a hall. Pleasant walking through fields and along the Tyne banks adds to the tally another Saxon church at Ovingham and an impressive Norman castle at Prudhoe. However, this area was also the heart of the Tyneside industrial revolution. Witnesses to this are old waggonway lines and an interesting assortment of bridges. Wylam can claim three of the greatest railway pioneers as residents. The Tyne valley countryside is very attractive even though you skirt industrial and residential areas. At Cherryburn and Ovingham you meet up with the great illustrator Thomas Bewick.

The **Fox and Hounds** in Wylam offers a reasonably priced full menu all week. Real ales are Jennings and Black Sheep. (The Boathouse Inn beside the station boasts twelve real ales.) A typical menu might include fillet of beef sautéed and finished in peppercorn sauce, strips of beef fillet flamed with brandy and finished in stroganoff sauce, smoked fillet of haddock in grain mustard sauce, king prawns sautéed in garlic butter, and lamb shank braised in port and rosemary sauce. There is also a good range of desserts. The inn is 'open plan' and has a relaxed atmosphere.

The Fox and Hounds is open from 12 noon to 11 pm. Food is available Tuesday to Saturday from 12 noon to 2 pm and 6 pm to 9 pm. Sunday lunch is from 12 noon to 4 pm.

Telephone: *01661 853246*

Note also the White Swan in Ovingham (*telephone: 01661 833188*) and Winships in Ovington (*telephone: 01661 835099*).

 The Walk

1 At **Bywell**, walk past cottages towards the castle. Beyond the entrance follow the footpath sign to **Bywell Bridge** through a wicket gate and along an enclosed path through a kissing gate onto a road. Turn right and cross Bywell Bridge. Walk along the road past **Stocksfield Hall**. At **Stocksfield Railway Station** turn left onto the platform, cross the footbridge to the car park and exit onto a road. Turn left and walk along the road past cottages, **Broomley County First School** and the **Stocksfield sports fields**. Just past the latter, turn left along a lane.

2 Follow the gated lane past **Merry Shield** then on along a track. Faced by two wide gates take the right-hand one. Keep on through a metal wicket gate then along a grassy track into woods. Cross two stiles by wide gates. After the second, cross a stile on the right into a field turning left to follow the path over a small hill past a waymarked post. Follow the track round to cross a ladder stile and follow the right field edge. At the end cross a stile, turn right then left to go through a wide gate and past **Eltringham Farm** onto a road. Up to the right is the entrance to **Cherryburn**. Turn left to continue the walk.

It was at Cherryburn (National Trust) that the great, and self taught, engraver Thomas Bewick was born in 1753: 'Cherryburn House, the place of my nativity, and which for many years my eyes beheld with cherished delight, is situated on the south side of the Tyne ... a short distance from the river.' Much of the inspiration for his work came from his childhood familiarity with the birds, animals and landscape of the area. He became not only an accomplished artist and engraver but also a naturalist, ornithologist and philosopher. He engraved the blocks for the famous History of Quadrapeds *and the* History of British Birds.

3 Walk downhill. At a cross-tracks turn right along a byway to **Eltringham** past a footpath sign to Prudhoe. Exit onto the busy A695 near the Hammerite paint factory. Cross the road and go through a wooden barrier. Now you have a ¾ mile stretch along **Castle Road**. At a road junction turn left then right into the lane to **Prudhoe Castle**. Walk down to a stone bridge ignoring a footpath sign on the right. Across the bridge turn left at a footpath sign for Hagg Bank. Keep on past **Prudhoe Mill** on the left. At a fork take the path to the right. At a path junction, keep left. Cross a footbridge and keep on. At another T-junction near the road turn right and keep on until you arrive at a new road. Cross this then at a three-way signpost turn down a path to Hagg Bank.

Prudhoe Castle was built in the late Norman period by Odinel de Umfraville, probably on the site of an older timber structure. Later it became the property of the Percys. It has an excellent defensive position, standing on a steep slope above the Tyne with a deep ravine to the east. A dry moat was added to the west and south. It is notable for its complex gateway and barbican and for the remains of what must have been an impressive keep with walls 10 ft thick.

4 At a path fork keep right. At the next fork, go left. When you arrive at the main road go through a wicket gate and cross over. Keep on down a footpath through the woods to a T-junction with a track. Turn right and walk ahead to a minor road. Turn left and at **Hagg Bank** cross a railway bridge. Near a telephone box turn right along **Hadrian's Cycleway** alongside the railway. Cross the **Hagg Bank Bridge**. Keep ahead along the old **Wylam Waggonway**. Go under a bridge and then through a tunnel. After this turn left up a path into **Falcon Terrace**. Turn left for the **Fox and Hounds**.

The Wylam Waggonway, built c1748, carried coal from Wylam Colliery to Lemington Staiths. The railway pioneers William Hedley and George Stephenson lived and worked in this area. Both Stephenson and Timothy Hackworth were born in Wylam. In 1808 cast-iron plate rails replaced wooden rails. In 1812 Wylam colliery employee William Hedley was asked by the owner, Christopher Blackett, to build a locomotive. A test version was running in 1813 and steam locomotives were well established by 1815. Wylam's name derives from Old English wil, a mechanical device or fish trap (related to our modern word wile), and could mean a watermill on a meadow (hamm).

THE 17TH-CENTURY PACKHORSE BRIDGE AT OVINGHAM

5 From the **Fox and Hounds** walk down the bank. Just before **Wylam Bridge** turn right along **Tyne View** then follow a riverside path. Stay with the upper path. At a former pit heap skirt to the right to rejoin the path. Keep on to cross the **Hagg Bank Bridge** and return to **Hagg Bank**. Just before the modern railway bridge turn right into the **Tyne Riverside Country Park**. Descend steps, cross a footbridge and keep on. Ignore paths to the left and keep on through two kissing gates. To the left you can see large chalk hills known as the **Spetchells**. At a fork keep left on a grassy path through gorse to join a metalled track. Stay

with this until it emerges into open country opposite **Ovingham**. Go beneath **Ovingham Bridge** then turn left into the Tyne Riverside car park and left to reach the road. Cross the footbridge.

6 Walk up into **Ovingham**. Turn left and follow the road past the church and the **Bridge End Inn**. Just past Ovingham's scenic packhorse bridge turn left at the footpath sign to River Tyne and follow the grass path to join a track. Follow this on as it narrows into a pleasant riverside path. Pass a waymarked path to the right and keep on across a couple of bridges to emerge into a village of chalets. Follow the track ahead

115

between chalets, at first with the river close on the left and then turning away to the right. Beyond the chalet village the track continues between fields then exits to a road via a gate at a road junction. Turn left and walk up to **Ovington**.

Ovingham church has a Saxon tower built in about 1050 which has classic Saxon features. The rest of this fine building is 13th- and 14th-century. Thomas Bewick's gravestone is displayed in the porch which he often decorated with chalk drawings. Bewick was educated at the school attached to Ovingham vicarage, as was Robert Surtees, the sporting novelist. There is also a very picturesque 17th-century packhorse bridge spanning the Whittle Burn, whose waters were once famous for bleaching linen.

7 In **Ovington** bear left past **Winships**. At the next left turning (**Burnside**), turn left and cross a stone stile on the right next to a wide gate. Descend the steep field to cross a stile in the far right corner then follow the right field edge to cross a

footbridge and stile. Keep on slightly to the left to cross another stile then traverse the next field in roughly the same direction to cross a stile near the right end of woodland. Cross the next field and cross another stile in a hedge. Follow the left field edge to cross a ladder stile. Bear half right to exit from this field via another ladder stile onto a road. Turn right past **Bywell Bridge** and return to **Bywell**.

Bywell is among the loveliest and most secluded places in Northumberland. Being within a loop of the Tyne it has a history of extreme flooding, hence the very visible flood defences. The great gatehouse of Bywell Castle was built in 1430 by Ralph Nevill, Earl of Westmorland. There was once a village here, although all that survives now is the village cross. Bywell Hall was built by James Paine in 1776. There are two churches because at Bywell two estates met, the Bolbecs and the Balliols. Both pre-date the Conquest. St Andrew's, founded by Walter of Bolbec, is especially notable for its Saxon tower.

Date walk completed:

ALLENDALE TOWN, SINDERHOPE, THE EAST ALLEN AND CATTON

THE FOOTBRIDGE NEAR SINDERHOPE

Distance:
11 miles

Map: OS Explorer OL 43 Hadrian's Wall

Starting Point:
Allendale Town
market place near
the King's Head.
GR 837558

How to get there: *Allendale Town is 11 miles to the south-west of Hexham on the B6295 which links the A686/A69 and the A689. The King's Head is on the north edge of the market place.*

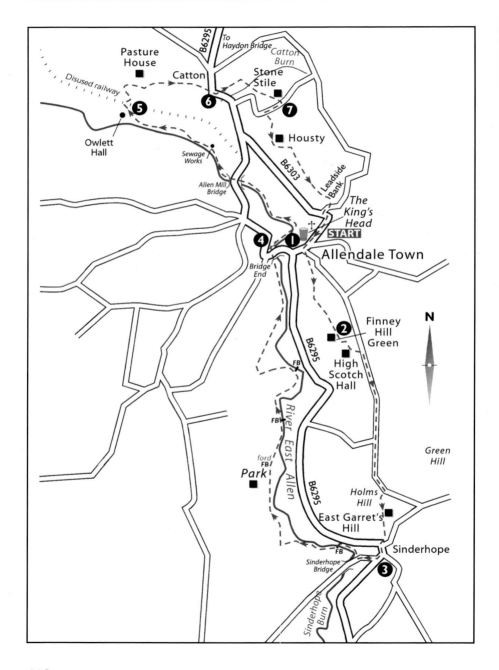

*T*he central feature of this walk is the pleasant Allendale Town, once the capital of this former lead mining area. There are various reminders of this industry albeit in a very attractive rural setting. Allendale is a claimant to the title of 'the centre of Britain' incidentally. Your companion for much of the way is the bubbling East Allen river. The outward section takes you up above the valley so you can enjoy some splendid views. From the hamlet of Sinderhope you follow the river closely to the East Allen bridge, which just happens to be a few hundred yards from the friendly King's Head. Then on through pleasant fields via Catton to return to Allendale.

Originally a coaching inn, with stables and outhouses at the rear, the **King's Head** is more than 300 years old. The stone floors and beams are original. With its dark, intimate interior and real fire, it exudes character. Friendly staff contribute to the sense that this is a genuine village 'local'. The main beers are Jenning's Cumberland Ale, Marston's Pedigree and Banks's Original. A good range of sandwiches and large filled rolls are available, as well as reasonably priced wholesome meals of good quality – the usual selection of steak, gammon, chicken, scampi, haddock and roast beef. There is also accommodation.

The King's Head is open from 11 am to 11 pm. Food is served between 12 noon and 2.30 pm and 6.30 pm and 9 pm.

Telephone: *01434 683681*; www.kingsheadallendale.com

Also note the Crown at Catton, open Monday and Wednesday to Saturday 12 noon to 11 pm, Tuesday 5 pm to 11 pm, Sunday 12 noon to 10 pm. *Telephone: 01434 683447*

The Walk

❶ From the **King's Head** walk down past the Co-op and cross the road beside Lloyds Bank. In the wall opposite is **Isaac's Well** (also known as the Bobbies' Well because it stands outside the former police station). Ascend the flight of steps next to it and follow the path between houses and a playground. Cross the road to the Finney Hill Green signpost. Walk up a short enclosed path to go through a gap into the field. Bear half right and cross a series of four fields up a slope, over a series of four waymarked stiles then a private drive and another stile. Continue with a wall to your right to cross a ladder stile (with a gap next to it). Continue with the wall to your right to cross a stone stile onto the drive of **Finney Hill Green Farm**.

Allendale Town stands in spectacular scenery at the geographical centre of Britain. Once the lead-mining capital, writer William Weaver Tomlinson described it in 1888 as 'a straggling dreary-looking place'. Its irregular market place is the scene of the famous Baal Fire celebration on New Year's Eve when 'guysers' dress up, blacken their faces and carry blazing tar barrels round the town on their heads. At midnight a huge bonfire is lit. The church of St Cuthbert (1873) is worth a visit. A memorial in the churchyard and Isaac's Well (1849) by the main road commemorate Isaac Holden, an itinerant tea seller renowned for his good works for the Allendale community.

❷ Turn right along the drive. Cross a stile by two gates and enter a field. Bear left towards **High Scotch Hall**. Cross stone stile then follow the field wall round crossing a stone stile on the left into a lane. Turn right and

walk between the farm buildings to exit onto a road. Turn right along this, passing a lane on your right, to **Studdon**. After the road bends between **Holms Hill** and **Green Hill** go through a wicket gate on the right (signed Sinderhope) near a black barn. Walk between walls for a few yards then turn left and walk downhill past a copse on the left. Continue round to the right and cross a wooden stile. Descend over pasture to a stile to the right of some Scots pine trees near **East Garret's Hill Farm**. Cross the stile and then the large field diagonally to the right corner. Exit onto the B6295 at **Sinderhope**.

❸ Cross **Sinderhope Bridge** then turn right along a lane. At a sign to Crowberry Hall on the right go through a kissing gate. Follow the path alongside the **East Allen** to go through another kissing gate then cross a footbridge. Turn right towards a ruined farm. Cross a stone stile behind it. From here follow the river on a clearly marked path. It is diverted leftwards in a meadow before a small patch of woodland and ascends a slope. Continue from a fingerpost passing **Park Farm** and the end of a metal bridge. Continue past a second footbridge then ascend a flight of steps past a house on the right. Exit into a field through a wicket gate. Bear right up the slope to the right and cross a stile on the right. Turn right to cross a ladder stile. Follow the waymarks again, with the river now far below you. Go through a white gate onto a road near restored buildings at **Bridge End**. Walk into **Allendale Town** if you want to visit the **King's Head**.

THE 300-YEAR-OLD PUB AT THE START OF THE WALK

❹ Return to **East Allen Bridge** then turn right at a sign to Allenmill/Oakpool. Embark on the riverside track, crossing a footbridge where water from the 4½ mile Blackett Level joins a stream entering the East Allen. Keep on past a ruined railway bridge abutment and across the road at **Allen Mill Bridge**. Follow the bridleway signed to Catton to pass sewage works then descend steps on the left to continue on the path closer to the river. Keep on over a stile and footbridges and through a wall gap by thick gorse. Cross another stile and follow the narrow path as it winds through thickening woodland and crosses another plank bridge. You reach a flight of steps on the right.

In 1729 Sir William Blackett opened Allenheads mine. The Blackett mines once yielded a seventh of the lead ore produced in the UK. By the late 19th century the industry was declining and Allendale lost half of its population between 1861 and 1901. The

Allenmill abutment which is passed on this walk was part of the railway carrying refined lead from the Allen valleys to Newcastle. Allen Mill was a smelting mill which is being restored. A huge waterwheel drove crushing equipment and furnaces burnt ore around the clock. Underground flues took the fumes away to the Allendale chimneys about three miles away.

❺ Ascend the steps up the valley side. Exit into a field over a stile. Follow the left field edge to cross a ladder stile. Cross the field diagonally right to **Owlet Hall**, a barn. Turn right through a gap in the fence. Cross a railway track and turn right through a gate into a field. Cross this half left up a steep slope to cross a stile and footbridge onto a track joining a road at **Struthers**. At the footpath sign turn right to Catton through the metal gate. Bear half right across the field to cross a composite stile obscured by a bend in the wall. The farm on your left is **Pasture House**. Follow the left field edge to the wall end. Go left through one metal gate then sharp right through another. Follow the enclosed path to **Catton**. At the end cross a step stile and a footbridge then go between houses into Catton centre.

Place names developed very much as a form of mental mapping with many of them being related to some sort of physical feature. Catton could mean wild-cat valley since the earliest spelling was Catteden – so watch your back. River names are usually pre-Roman. The original spelling of Allen was Alwent and probably meant white or clear. Housty, later on this route, was originally spelt Howsepette and meant path along which hogs were driven, but later became a corrupted form of hog-sty. Sinderhope means southern valley.

6 At the telephone kiosk cross the road to a sign to **Stone Stile**. Follow the lane through a metal gate, past a large cow barn then through another two gates and across a field. Climb a ladder stile then cross another field and cross another stile. After the second stile turn right and follow

the wall on the right to cross a footbridge over **Catton Burn**. Cross a high stile on the left. Now follow a slight stream on your right up to a track. Turn right and go through a gate. Turn left to go through another gate then up to cross a stone stile. Head for the farm and cross a ladder stile to the right of the buildings. Bear left round the buildings to the drive and thence a lane.

7 Turn right down the lane then left at a sign to **Housty**, past a ruined barn. Bear round to the right of the farm and cross a stone stile on the left. Keep on left to a waymarked gate. The footpath has been diverted here. Go through into a field then turn left and round to a ladder stile. Cross this then turn right and follow the wall on the right. Go through a gate onto a track. Turn right then, within yards, through a gate on the left. Now follow a path over a very large field with the wall on your left. At a wall corner keep on, bearing slightly left to cross a ladder stile. Turn right following the wall on your right to cross a stile into a narrow path to a gate. Exit onto **Leadside Bank** where you turn right to the main road and return to **Allendale**.

Date walk completed:

WHITLEY CHAPEL, DIPTON DENE, DIPTONMILL AND DYE HOUSE

THE ROWLEY BURN AT WHITLEY MILL

Distance:
12 miles

Map: OS Explorer OL 43 Hadrian's Wall

Starting Point:
Whitley Chapel
parish hall.
GR 927578

How to get there: *Whitley Chapel is 4 miles south of Hexham on a minor road leading from the B6306 (to Blanchland). Take a side lane signed Whitley Mill and park beside the parish hall and sports fields in a designated parking area.*

123

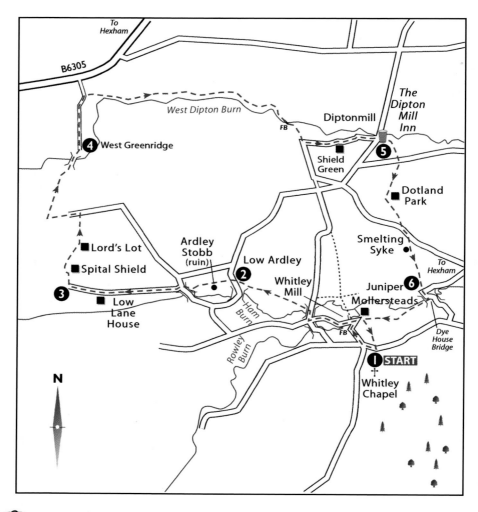

The **Dipton Mill Inn** is also the tap for the Hexhamshire Brewery. It was built on the site of an old farmhouse and mill which burnt down in the 1780s. It is intimate, stone-floored and has a beamed ceiling and a real fire in winter. There is a large garden with a stream running through it. Beers include Hexhamshire Devil's Elbow, Shire Bitter, Devil's Water, Whapweasel and Old Humbug. A wide variety of sandwiches and salads are available. Ploughman's lunch involves selecting from 14 cheeses, including most of the Northumbrian varieties. Food is home-cooked from local ingredients and served with fresh vegetables. A typical menu includes such items as haddock baked with tomato and basil, steak and kidney pie, chicken breast in sherry sauce and bacon chops in cider sauce. There are also home-made sweets such as fruit crumble, lemon tart and chocolate and rum truffle tart.

The Dipton Mill Inn is open from 12 noon to 2.30 pm and 6 pm to 11 pm Monday to Saturday, and 12 noon to 3 pm and 7 pm to 10.30 pm on Sunday. Food is available daily between 12 noon and 2.30 pm and 6.30 pm to 8.30 pm.

Telephone: *01434 606577*; www.diptonmill.co.uk

---

*W*ithout the lovely three-mile stretch of woodland walking along the edge of deep Dipton Dene, the curious legend of the Queen's Cave and the robber 'Black Jack', the tragic tale of the Earls of Derwentwater, the unique taste of Hexhamshire Brewery beer and the tempting menu of the Dipton Mill Inn, this would be just an idyllic walk across quiet Hexhamshire pasture land and along field edges.

 *The Walk*

1 From the parking area walk past the playing field down the pleasant quiet lane to a ford across the **Rowley Burn** at **Whitley Mill**. Cross a footbridge and follow the lane on to a junction. Turn right down the road to Dotland/Channel Well/Hexham. Just over a bridge turn left, cross a stile then follow a rough path up to the left into a V-shaped field bounded by steep slopes on two sides. Keep ahead into the woodland fringe on the third side. Keep on through the woodland to carefully cross the difficult double stile in a fence corner. Keep straight ahead over four fields and through a series of gates to arrive in the farmyard of **Low Ardley**. Pass to the left of the farmhouse and join a road.

The Rowley Burn is a tributary of the famous Devil's Water which it joins near Juniper. The name is derived from a family called D'Eivill who held land here in the 12th century. Eventually their estates passed to the Radcliffes, the Earls of Derwentwater, who had a blood relationship with the Stuarts. They lived at Dilston, a corruption of Dyvelston. Their estates were confiscated following their participation in the 1715 Jacobite rebellion and James Radcliffe, Earl of Derwentwater was executed. His younger brother Charles escaped only to be recaptured on his way to join the 1745 rebellion, and he also was executed.

2 Turn right then left through a double field gate following the sign to **Ardley Stobb**. Pass in front of a house to go through a wide gate. Turn right and follow the right field edge then through a gate, near a ruined farm. Keep ahead over the field to cross a stile hidden in a dip. Then follow the left field edge to cross a ladder stile at the bottom of a steep bank. Turn right on a lane then left at a wooden cottage and walk up a lane passing **Low Lane House**. At the lane end, past a line of Scots pines, turn right down the track to **Spital Shield**. Follow it through the farmyard.

3 Keep ahead through a wide gate then half right across the field and through another gate. Bear right down the steep hill and descend to cross carefully an old stone step stile. Cross a little burn as best you can. Across the burn, walk up the steep slope, then in front of **Lord's Lot**, meet a track and turn left through a gate. Turn right up the farm drive to a T-junction. Turn left and go through a wide gate (signed Allendale Town/Catton) onto

moorland. Follow the wall on your right. At the end of the wall turn right. Now follow a pleasant gated track to **West Greenridge** with its prominent monkey puzzle tree.

Lord's Lot has no biblical significance. It dates back to the period of enclosures in the 18th century and occasional land distribution by lottery. So this was a section which went to the Lord of the Manor. Ardley is named after a Saxon called Earda, while -ley means clearing. This was Earda's Clearing, in a once heavily wooded area. Ardley Stobb implies the difficulty of clearance because the word stobb (stump or post) indicates that this was an area of tree stumps. Spital is a corruption of hospital (meaning a hostel in this context). Shield suggests there was a shepherd's summer pasture shelter. So Spital Shield refers to a refuge for travellers where there was also a shepherd's hut at some time.

4 Follow the lane to a signpost on the right saying 'Diptonmill 3 miles'. Turn right and start this long woodland stretch on a clear, undulating path. There is a wall on the left to begin with and the burn is far below. At a marked bridleway fork, keep right. Ignore all paths to the left. Eventually the path descends, becoming quite rocky and sunken and sometimes slippery. It bends to the right as you approach the valley floor. Near the stream at a waymarker turn left then cross a footbridge. Walk up a steep rocky track which turns right and levels out then reaches a lane. Turn left and follow this past **Shield Green Nurseries** to a junction at **Diptonmill**.

THE LEAFY DIPTON MILL INN

The Battle of Hexham took place in 1464 during the Wars of the Roses. Following the defeat, Queen Margaret fled with her son Edward, the Prince of Wales. She made her way by chance to Dipton where she encountered robbers. She persuaded their leader to look after them. He lodged them temporarily in a cave in the dene – roughly 30 ft long and about 14 ft high. Not far away is a house called Queen's Letch, and it is claimed that it was there that her horse slipped and that she had to continue on foot. The word letch implies a boggy patch or a slow running stream in marsh. Dipton is a corruption of the original name Depedene – which it is of course.

⑤ From the **Dipton Mill Inn** cross the road and follow the muddy track to meet a road. Cross the road by a sign to Smelting Syke and follow the track up to **Dotland Park**. Bend right past barns then pens and go through one wide field gate then another, then bear half right across the big field towards the left corner and a new plantation. Cross a stream using an earth and stone bridge and then cross a ladder stile onto a road. Turn left and go past a drive (the right of way has been legally diverted here). Go through a waymarked wicket gate on the right signed **Juniper**. Cross the field to go through another wicket gate. Follow the left field edge through a kissing gate and down an enclosed path. Through another wicket gate keep on down the next left field edge. At the wall end cross a stile on the right, partly hidden by a hedge, and exit onto a road. Cross over to go through another wicket gate and cross the field. Go through another kissing gate and down an enclosed path onto a road.

6 Turn right through **Dye House**. Across a bridge turn right along a footpath following the woodland edge and stream. At a section of broken wall the path goes behind briefly to avoid a section of eroded bank. Cross a stone bridge over a side stream and after a few yards turn left into the woods following markers. The path rises sharply to a stile. Cross this then turn right along the field edge to a wicket gate. Go through, then cross a stile opposite. Follow the right field edge to go through a field gate on the right. Through this bear slightly left to go through another wide gate. At **Mollersteads** farm turn left and walk past a small wooded hill. At a marker post keep half right and avoid a boggy hollow by staying on a bank with old fence posts on your

left. Cross a ladder stile then follow a fence to exit onto a road across a stile and down steps. Turn right and walk past **St Helen's church** into **Whitley Chapel**.

Dotland is a name of Scandinavian origin dating from at least 1160 and refers to one Dote. *The origin of Juniper is obvious enough although it was once spelt as* Giniper, *which explains why* Gin *is so called. Dye House is more modern. It relates to the once thriving glove trade of Hexhamshire. Mollersteads was obviously noteworthy for mallow plants which were used in dyeing. Whitley Chapel takes its name from a chapel or oratory which existed here in medieval times. It was rebuilt in the 17th century. The local Quakers held their meetings on Chapel Hill. The present St Helen's church was founded in 1760. The* Whitley *section may be because this was a cleared area or* ley *which happened to be lighter than the forested area around it, hence the* whit *or* white *which is quite a common place name element.*

Date walk completed: